Beginner's Guide to
Stumpwork

This book is dedicated to my parents and my husband
Michael, all of whom have encouraged me throughout my life.
This is a special dedication to my Mum, who so much wanted
to see this book; sadly she passed away before it was published.

Beginner's Guide to
Stumpwork

Kay Dennis

SEARCH PRESS

First published in Great Britain 2001

Search Press Limited
Wellwood, North Farm Road,
Tunbridge Wells, Kent TN2 3DR

ISBN 0 85532 870 3

Suppliers
If you have any difficulty in obtaining any of the materials and equipment mentioned in this book, then please write to the publishers for a current list of stockists, which includes firms who operate a mail-order service:

Search Press Limited, Wellwood,
North Farm Road, Tunbridge Wells,
Kent TN2 3DR, England

I would like to acknowledge the help, tuition and friendship given to me over the years by my tutors and students, and by the team at Search Press.

Most of all, I would like to thank Pat Gibson, and Barbara and Roy Hirst, who were instrumental in getting me thoroughly involved in needlelace and stumpwork.

If it had not been for all these people I would never have written this book.

Printed in Spain by Elkar S. Coop. Bilbao 48012

Contents

INTRODUCTION

Stumpwork dates from the 17th Century, and like all seventeenth-century embroiderers, I was introduced to embroidery at an early age. My great aunt taught me the easy stitches, then, at school, my teachers encouraged me in a subject I obviously enjoyed and excelled in.

In the late 1960s I attended a textile course, where I was introduced to the technique of needlelace. I only made a small leaf shape, but I enjoyed making it so much that I decided to explore the techniques further. Although I still practised embroidery, I began to love needlelace and all its possibilities.

Two decades on I found stumpwork, which meant I could combine my two passions – embroidery and needlelace – bliss! My stumpwork tutors, Barbara and Roy Hirst, not only taught me the techniques but instilled in me a love and appreciation for this complex but fascinating style of embroidery. I began teaching needlelace in 1984 and stumpwork in 1994, and my enthusiasm for both these crafts is still strong – I just love stitching.

In recent years my work has changed, largely due to my teaching activities; I have explored new threads and materials, and different ways of using them. Although I still like to embroider in a traditional style, my work has taken on a more contemporary appearance. I tried using a sewing machine, but hand stitching is my first love.

Traditional stumpwork is small, intricate and, sometimes, frustrating to make. But – once hooked – you will look at embroidery differently, and you may even find that flat needlework looks uninteresting.

Stumpwork is sometimes confused with the Elizabethan style of padded embroidery. Both types of work are raised, but the styles are completely different. The Elizabethan style generally has scrolled patterns, in the form of coiling stems, with flowers and fruits, whereas the later stumpwork embroideries are more picturesque.

Stumpwork is currently enjoying a revival largely due to Barbara Hirst, who, having discovered this delightful form of embroidery in 1980, started to teach and demonstrate it around the world. It grows everpopular with embroiderers and lacemakers alike, who use both traditional materials and the extensive range of modern ones. A typical modern stumpwork embroidery contains flat, padded and freestanding embroidery, and slips (small pieces of needlework made on separate pieces of fabric).

Stumpwork is not as alarming as it might first appear. In this book, I have included projects that even someone new to embroidery can achieve with ease. I show you, step by step, how to make and use different types of padding, and the embroidery and needlelace stitches commonly used in stumpwork. When you get used to the stitches and techniques, try to develop your own ideas by experimenting with other modern materials.

This book is for all embroiderers who like to stitch by hand. I hope it will inspire those who have never attempted or even seen stumpwork before; encourage those who have worked a little and would like to know more; and interest those who want to make the projects for the sheer enjoyment of making something in a traditional way. No two stitchers interpret a design in the same way, so each embroidery becomes unique.

Finally, I would like to pass on a few tips which I found out about by accident! Put a cloth over your embroidery when you are not stitching to keep it clean; wash your hands before doing any embroidery and, most important of all, keep tea and coffee away from the work. I once tripped over an extension cable stretched across my workroom, spilt a cup of coffee and ruined several months' embroidery work!

Happy stitching.

History

Towards the end of the seventeenth century, this highly elaborate, intricate and decorative form of raised and padded embroidery became popular in Britain. It was used to decorate caskets, boxes, mirror frames, panels, book covers and pin cushions. Although new to England, a similar style of embroidery had been worked by professional European embroiderers for over a century.

Dictionaries define stumpwork as: 'elaborate raised embroidery of the 15th–17th centuries using various materials, and raised by stumps of wood or pads of wool'. In the 17th Century it was called raised or embossed work. Later, it became known as embroidery on the stump, and the term stumpwork was first used in the

19th Century. We are not sure how the term came about, but it was probably because of the small stumps of wood used to raise parts of the embroidery.

Embroidery was an essential part of the education of young ladies of the time, and they worked samplers in canvaswork, whitework, needlelace and beadwork. The samplers were often limited in design, so, having mastered the basic skills, the ladies wanted to use them in a less restrictive way. Imagine their delight in selecting materials, threads and patterns, then working something new and exciting.

Embroiderers did not create their own designs; they had an endless source of

British stumpwork box, circa 1650, gifted to the Embroiderers' Guild Museum Collection, Hampton Court Palace, by Miss Hester Clough.

Enlarged detail taken from the stumpwork opposite.

material in contemporary pattern books, woodcuts and engravings. Having chosen a pattern, the embroiderer would employ a professional printmaker to paint or print the design on to a silk or satin background. A typical example of period stumpwork would include human figures, mythological figures, animals, castles, flowers, fruits and insects, filling every space. No attention was paid to scale; the motifs were often disproportionate in size to each other.

The embroiderers would possibly have worked from kits containing most of the materials they needed, including small, ready-formed pieces of wood (probably boxwood) in the shape of fruit, hands and heads to be covered with stitching.

Other materials would include gold threads, dyed silk and chenille threads and fabrics, metal purl, beads, pearls, semi-precious stones, hair and feathers. Wires and vellum, bound with silk, were used to provide further textural and decorative detail.

On completion the embroidery would be sent to a cabinetmaker to be mounted on to a casket or mirror frame.

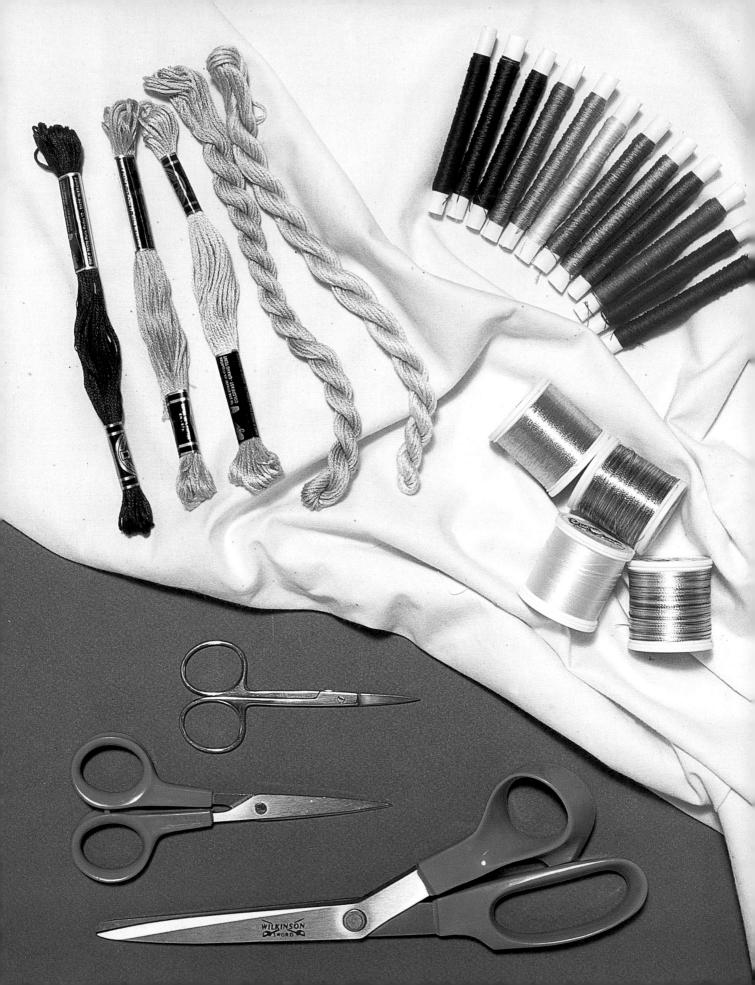

Materials

The materials used in stumpwork are generally available from good needlework shops. Specialist materials are available from mail order outlets who advertise in the needlework magazines.

Fabrics

A plain background fabric, strong enough to support the sometimes heavily padded and wired elements should be used for stumpwork. A good quality, medium-weight calico is suitable for most projects, although silk with a backing of calico, is also suitable. When setting up an embroidery project, allow sufficient fabric all round the design for mounting in a hoop and for final framing.

Medium-weight calico is also ideal for use as the backing fabric in needlelace pads.

Lightweight calico, which folds more easily, is best for making slips and stuffed pads for faces.

Threads

There is a very wide range of threads that can be used in stumpwork – cotton, silk, metallic, synthetic and wool, all in hundreds of different colours and textures – each creating a different result. With experience you will be able to select the correct thread for the effect you want to achieve. Try to use the finest threads, 100/3 silks or one strand of six-stranded cotton. I often use space-dyed threads to create interesting finishes; I prefer to use hand-dyed threads rather than machine-dyed ones as the latter can end up being too stripey.

I use a fine, strong crochet cotton No. 80 for needle-lace cordonnets, in a colour to match that of the filling stitch thread.

I only use sewing thread for work that is not going to be visible in the finished embroidery; for securing pads and for couching down the cordonnet threads.

Scissors

Always use sharp scissors. You will need a large pair for cutting fabrics, a general-purpose pair for cutting paper, wire, etc., and a small, very sharp pair for cutting threads.

Needles

Use the needle appropriate for the purpose. It should pass through the fabric easily, and it should have an eye large enough to take the thread comfortably, but not so big that the thread keeps falling out. I regularly use three types of needle for stumpwork:

Crewel or embroidery needles for all embroidery stitches. They have long eyes and sharp points.

Sharps needles for all general sewing.

Ballpoint needles for making needlelace and for making stitches on top of each other.

I also use beading needles for adding decorative beads to my embroideries, and a large, tapestry needle to help make cordonnets.

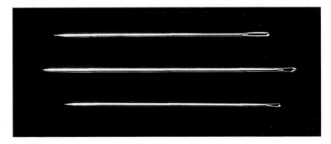

Crewel, ballpoint and sharps needles.

Padding materials

Interfacing This is a fabric stiffener available in different grades and thicknesses. I use a firm, heavyweight grade for raising flat surfaces. I colour it with fabric paints.

Felt This comes in different thicknesses and grades, and in lots of colours. Use a smooth, thin felt in a colour that matches the embroidery threads for more rounded shapes. Pads can be made using layers of felt applied over each other, or by stuffing a single layer of felt with toy stuffing.

Toy stuffing Use a polyester toy stuffing, as it pulls out to almost single strands and can be pushed into the smallest of spaces. Kapok stuffing tends to be lumpy and it can be difficult to fill a space evenly. Quilters' wadding is not suitable for stumpwork.

Cotton moulds These are available from craft or hobby shops, and are ideal for making apples, oranges, etc. They should be painted before being covered with thread. Balsa wood is a good alternative to cotton moulds; it is a very soft wood that can be sculpted with a craft knife.

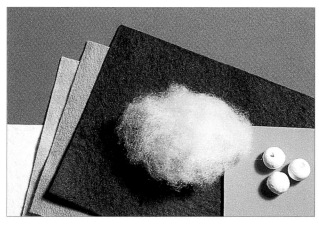

Interfacing, felt, toy stuffing and cotton moulds.

Embroidery frames

Mounting the background fabric in a frame will help keep a good tension on your work.

Circular embroidery hoops are available in many sizes and are very easy to use. The background fabric is supported between two concentric rings, the outer one of which usually has a screwed clamp.

Slate frames are equally as good, especially for large embroideries, but you do have to stretch and sew the background fabric to the frame.

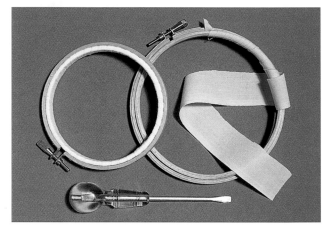

The inner ring of circular embroidery hoops should be bound with strips of cotton (see page 15).

An adjustable floor, or table-top, frame stand will free up both hands and help to eliminate back ache and strain.

Other equipment

The following items are not essential for stumpwork, but they will allow you to explore its full potential.

Glue I use PVA glue to secure toy stuffing in open-ended felt pads and to secure silk thread when wrapping wire.

Thimble Especially useful when sewing through leather and similar materials.

Horsehair I use this to strengthen the outlines of needlelace shapes that are to be freestanding.

Wire I incorporate fine wire in the top stitching of some pieces of needlelace to allow them to be bent into shape. I wrap paper-covered wire with silk thread to form flower stalks and the hands of figures.

Cocktail sticks I use these to help fill felt pads with toy stuffing. They can also be used to create accessories for embroidery designs.

Stiletto This sharp, pointed tool is used for making small holes in fabric.

Tweezers Useful for intricate work and for removing small trimmings of thread.

Beads Tiny beads or buttons can be used to decorate embroideries. Others can be wrapped in much the same way as cotton moulds.

Some of the other equipment I use for my stumpwork embroideries.

Felt pens and pencils For sketching and for drawing paper patterns.

Air-drying clay Not essential, but useful for creating special shapes such as flowerpots.

Fabric paint and brushes I use fabric paint to colour interfacing pads, cotton moulds and fabric slips before embroidering over these, and to paint the backgrounds for landscape designs. I use gold fabric paint to outline shapes on background fabrics before applying pads or stitches.

Acrylic paints I use these to colour wooden beads and other non-fabric items used in my designs.

Dressmakers' pins For holding pads down on the background fabric before sewing them in place.

Silk frame and silk pins For stretching fabric before it is painted.

Paper I use tracing paper to transfer designs on to plain paper patterns.

Self-adhesive, transparent plastic This is ideal as the protective layer in needlelace pads. I actually use a transparent fabric known as architect's linen, but this is not readily available.

Getting started

In this section, I explain a few simple tasks that must be performed before you start to work on an embroidery. First, you have to work up your design and create a full-size paper pattern. Then you must transfer it to the background fabric, prepare your embroidery hoop and mount the background fabric in it.

Creating a design

As a beginner, you can copy the designs from this book. Soon, however, you will want to create your own designs. So, where do you start? Well, there are lots of sources of inspiration.

Childrens' colouring books, magazines, greetings cards and postcards, for example, often have images that could – with a little imagination – be turned into a stumpwork embroidery. The law of copyright says that you cannot make exact copies of other people's designs without their permission, but there is nothing wrong with adapting them.

When you go out and about, take a small sketch book with you; even if you cannot sketch well, a simple drawing with notes of colours that you see will help remind you of a design idea.

Alternatively, you can get some very good results with a small, point-and-shoot camera. Shots of the whole scene, as well as details, could be useful in the future. Your family and friends will soon get used to you taking the most unusual pictures!

Try to find a natural subject with a shape or colour range which appeals to you – it could be a flower, a fungus, a rock, a bird, an insect or even some fruit – then make lots of sketches or take several photographs.

When you have your source material, start to work up a design. Use a photocopier to enlarge or reduce different images to the same scale. Break a complex subject into individual shapes – the calyx, petals, stalks and leaves of a flower, for example – and try to simplify the shape without losing its identity. Try putting some of the shapes together; a fungus growing on a tree-stump, or an insect sitting on a flower.

Gradually, you will start to look at the world around you in a different way. Something will catch your eye and you will find yourself saying: 'How can I recreate that in stumpwork?'

When you have chosen your subject, make a pencil sketch, simplifying the shapes as much as possible.

14

Preparing the background fabric

When you are happy with your design, make a full-size paper pattern. Cut the fabric to size, remembering to add an allowance for framing the finished work, fold it to find its centre, then mark this point with a pin.

Place the pin over the centre of the paper pattern and transfer the design on to the fabric. I follow the traditional method and use a fine brush and gold fabric paint to draw outlines on to fabric. You only need to transfer the basic outlines of the design, as all detail will be covered by stitches. Do

not transfer the outlines of any freestanding elements of your embroidery, or they will show. When the paint is completely dry, use an iron to 'heat set' it.

Hoop frames are more than adequate for the projects in this book. Use hoops 5cm (2in) larger all round than the design. If you have to use a small frame with a large design, work the design area by area.

Most hoop frames have a tightening mechanism, but the embroidery fabric can still slip. Binding the inner ring with strips

of cotton sheeting cut on the bias will keep the fabric taut.

Centre the design over the bound inner ring then clamp it with the outer one. Fine fabrics, such as silk or lightweight calico, will not support the weight of stumpwork on their own, so I mount a piece of medium-weight calico behind these.

Remove the fabric from the frame when you finish a needle-work session; if the fabric is left in the frame for long periods of time, the rings may cause marks which can be difficult to remove.

Fold the fabric in half, then in half again to find the centre point. Mark this with a dressmaker's pin.

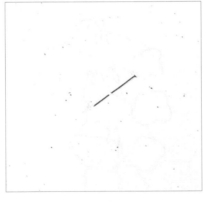

Open up the fabric, then centre it over the design. A lightbox or a sunny window will help you position it.

Use a fine brush and gold fabric paint to transfer the outlines of the design from the pattern on to the fabric.

Bind the inner ring of hoop frames to help keep the fabric taut.

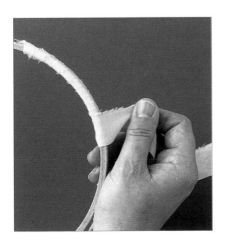

Place the fabric over the inner ring, press the outer ring over the top, tighten the clamp, then pull the fabric taut.

EMBROIDERY TECHNIQUES

In this chapter, I take you through the basic techniques of embroidered stumpwork. This sampler includes five projects and some small filler designs. Individual projects would make delightful embroideries on their own, and could be framed to make the perfect gift for someone special. The small designs, the patterns of which are included at the back of the book, could, for example, be used to decorate the lid of a box.

Each project is complete with step-by-step instructions to show you how to use different padding and raising techniques, and how to work the different stitches used to embroider it.

Flowing flowers

The padding used for the raised leaves and petals of this floral design are made from heavyweight interfacing. This is quite stiff, making it ideal for the crisp edges of leaves and petals. It also makes satin stitch easier to work as it helps guide the needle passing through the background fabric. I usually paint the interfacing to match the thread colour so that the eye is not distracted by any white peeping through the stitches. Interfacing accepts fabric paint easily, but let it dry overnight before using it.

Satin stitch covers all the leaves and flowers, stem stitch is used for the flower stalks and Turkey knot stitch forms the raised body of the butterfly. The wings of the butterfly, which stand proud of the surface, are worked in long and short stitch over wire couched down on a separate piece of fabric.

You will need:

Medium-weight calico
Fabric paint and brush
Heavyweight interfacing
Tracing paper and pencil
Sewing thread
Six-stranded cotton
No. 7 embroidery needle
Dressmakers' pins
Fine wire
Stiletto

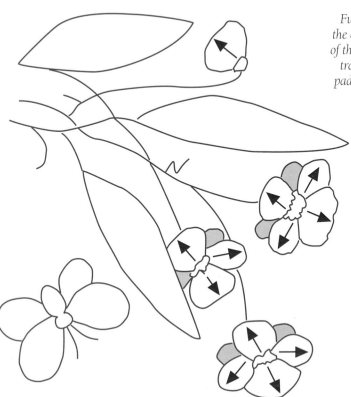

Full-size pattern. Use gold fabric paint to transfer the outlines on to the background fabric. The wings of the butterfly stand proud of the surface, so do not transfer these. The petals coloured in pink are not padded, and the arrows on the other petals indicate the direction of the satin stitches.

Preparing the padding

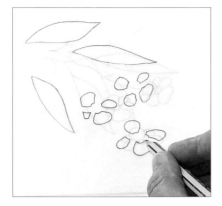

1. Transfer the outlines of the three leaves and the twelve petals shown here on to tracing paper, then cut out each shape. Keep the groups of petals together until you are ready to use them.

2. Use a green fabric paint to colour a piece of interfacing (the area must be large enough to cut out the three leaves).

3. Pin a tracing-paper leaf shape to the dry coloured interfacing, then cut out the shape.

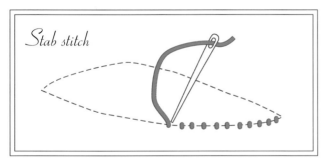

Stab stitch

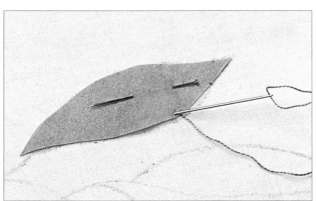

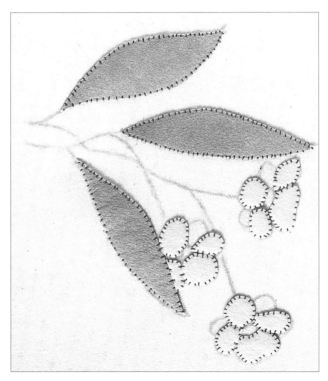

4. Pin the shape within its gold outline, then using a matching thread, stab stitch the leaf shape to the background fabric.

5. Cut out the other two leaves from the coloured interfacing, and the twelve petal shapes from white interfacing, then secure all the shapes to the background fabric.

Working the stalks

Stem stitch is used to work all the flower stalks. Use a No. 7 embroidery needle and one strand of six-stranded cotton thread. Work the longest stalks first, starting at the flower head or leaf end, then work the shorter stalks, blending them into the long ones.

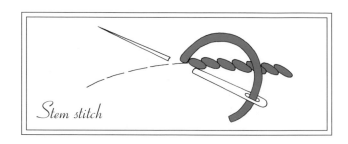

Stem stitch

  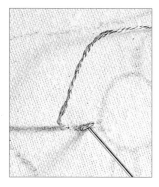 

1. Bring the needle and thread up through the fabric approximately 6mm (¹/₄in) from the start point of the stalk.

2. Take the needle down at the start point, then bring it back up again about 3mm (¹/₈in) beyond the first stitch.

3. Now take the needle down through the fabric, approximately halfway along the first stitch.

4. Bring the needle back up 3mm (¹/₈in) beyond the second stitch, then back down halfway along the second stitch. Continue working stitches until the stalk is complete.

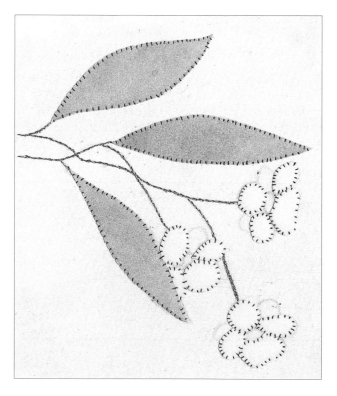

All stem-stitch stalks completed.

20

Working the leaves and petals

The leaves and petals are all embroidered in satin stitch using a No. 7 embroidery needle and one strand of six-stranded cotton.

I make the first stitch across the middle of the shape, work out to one side, then go back to the middle and work the other side.

The pink shapes on the diagram (see page 18) are not raised, and should be embroidered before working on the raised petals. Work the stitches from the centre of the flower outwards, generally in the direction of the arrows shown on the diagram.

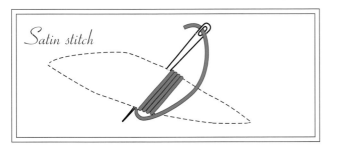

All satin stitches completed. Note that the centres of each flower head are filled with French knots (see page 30).

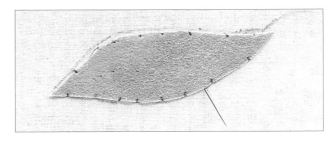

1. Bring the needle up through the fabric, one-third of the way along one side of the leaf shape.

2. Take the thread diagonally across the shape, hold it flat, then take the needle down through the fabric where the thread crosses the edge of the padding.

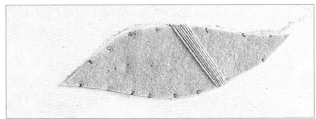

3. Bring the needle up at the right-hand side of the thread on the bottom edge of the padding, take it across the leaf, parallel to the first stitch, then back down through the fabric again. Continue working across the leaf shape.

4. When you have covered the right-hand side of the shape, work another series of satin stitches from the centre out to the left-hand side. Work the other leaves in a similar way. If worked carefully, satin stitch creates a wonderful sheen across the shape.

Working the butterfly

The body of the butterfly, which completes this project, is worked in Turkey knot stitch, using a No. 7 embroidery needle and two strands of six-stranded cotton. The resulting loops are trimmed off to create a fluffy raised area.

The wings are worked on a separate piece of calico. Fine wire formers are couched on to the fabric, then the enclosed shapes are worked with long and short stitches. These stitches are worked with one strand of six-stranded cotton.

For clarity, the step-by-step photographs for making the wings do not include the embroidered body.

Full-size pattern.

Turkey knot stitch

This stitch produces rows of secured loops which can then be trimmed to create a fluffy pile.

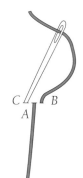

1. Insert the needle through fabric at A, leaving a tail of thread on the surface. Bring the needle up at B, then down at C; pull the thread tight to make a small securing stitch.

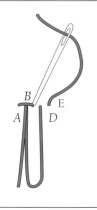

2. Bring the needle back up at A, then insert it at D, leaving a loop of thread on the surface. Bring the needle up at E, then down at B; again, pull the thread tight to make a securing stitch.

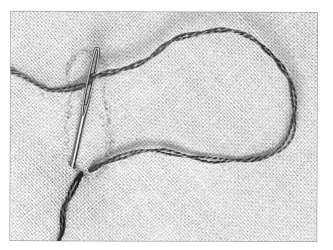

1. Starting at the bottom of the body, make the first knot leaving a short tail of thread on the surface.

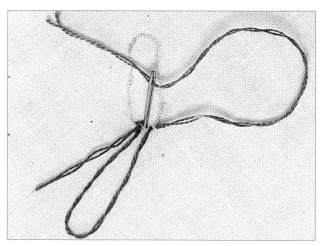

2. Tighten the knot, then, leaving a short loop on the surface, make another knot to one side.

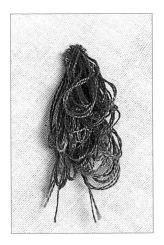

3. Take the thread across the back of the fabric, then bring it up just above the first row of knots. Make another row of knots, then, repeating this step, work up the body shape.

4. Continue making rows of knots until the body shape is completely filled with knots.

5. Use a sharp pair of scissors to trim off the loops to create a rounded fluffy pile.

6. Transfer the outline of the four wings on to a piece of lightweight calico with gold fabric paint, leaving space for cutting out each wing. Cut lengths of fine wire to fit the contour of each wing. Allow for two 25mm (1in) tails to support the wings when they are sewn on to the body.

Couching

Make couching stitches as invisible as possible by taking the needle up and down through the same hole in the background fabric.

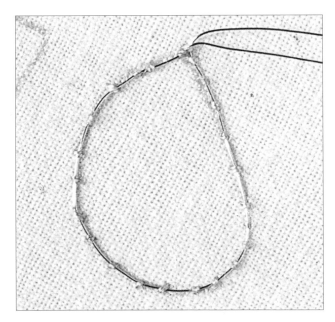

7. Couch the wire over the gold outlines.

Long and short stitch

On the second and subsequent rows of stitches, take the thread down through the end of the stitch on the previous row. This practice will give a very smooth finish to the stitches.

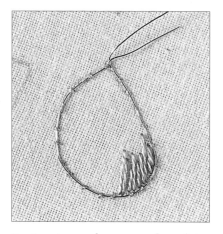

8. Starting at the outer edge of the wing shape, use one strand of six-stranded cotton and a No. 7 embroidery needle to make a series of long and short stitches alternately across the shape.

9. On the next and subsequent rows, bring the needle and thread up a short distance away from the first short stitch of the previous row, then take the thread through the end of this stitch and back into the background fabric.

Buttonhole stitch

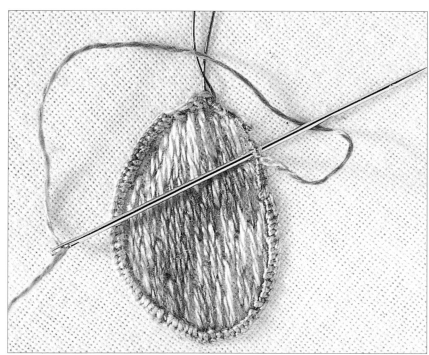

10. When the wing shape is completely filled with long and short stitch, work a hem of buttonhole stitches over the wire. Start at the base of the wing and work right round the shape. Do not cut off the excess thread as this is used to secure the wing to the body shape.

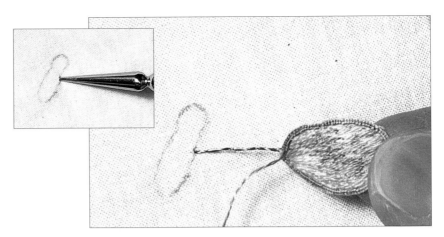

11. Cut round the outside edge, as close as possible to the buttonhole stitches.

12. Use a stiletto to make a small hole in the side of the body shape. Twist the wire tails together, then push them through the hole to the back of the fabric. Take the loose length of thread through the same hole.

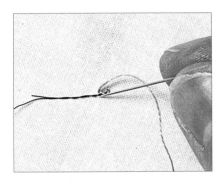

13. On the back of the fabric, fold the wire tail down the length of the body shape, then oversew it to secure it to the fabric. Repeat with the other three wings.

The finished embroidery.

Acorns

Felt, padded out with toy stuffing, is used to create the rounded appearance of the acorns in this project. The stalks are embroidered in stem stitch (see page 20), the leaves and the basic acorn shapes are worked in satin stitch (see page 21), then the tip of each acorn is finished with a small French knot (see page 30). Finally, the acorn cups are worked in Ceylon stitch, the texture of which is perfect for depicting the knobbly surface of the acorn cups.

You will need:

Medium-weight calico
Fabric paint and brush
Tracing paper and pencil
Felt
Toy stuffing
Cocktail sticks
Sewing thread
Six-stranded cotton
No. 7 embroidery needle

Stuffing the felt padding

Felt is a versatile padding material that can be stuffed to create rounded shapes for oversewing. Use a good quality fine felt, and select a colour that is compatible with the embroidery threads.

Cut the felt shapes so that they sit just inside the gold outline on the fabric. Stab stitches (see page 19) are used to secure the felt to the fabric; these should be very neat and as small as possible.

Take your time when stuffing the shapes; a smoother finish will be achieved by slowly building up the shape with small amounts of stuffing.

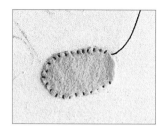

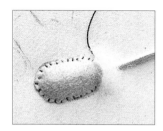

1. Stab stitch round the shape; bring the needle out of the fabric at an angle, then take it down through the edge of the felt. Leave a small gap.

2. Use a cocktail stick to push stuffing into the pouch. When you have achieved the required shape, close the gap with more stab stitches.

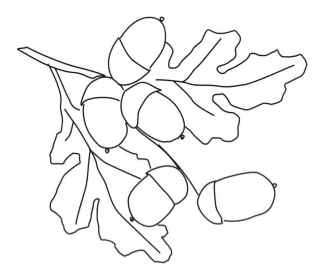

Full-size pattern. Use gold fabric paint to transfer all the outlines on to the background fabric.

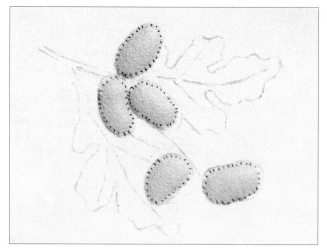

All padding stuffed and sewn on to the background fabric.

26

Working the acorns

Start the embroidery by using stem stitch and satin stitch to embroider the stalks and leaves respectively. Then, using a No. 7 embroidery needle and one strand of six-stranded cotton, cover the whole of each padded acorn shape with long satin stitches. Start in the middle of a shape, work across to one side, then go back and work the other side. Finish each acorn with a small French knot at the top. Now use the same needle and thread and Ceylon stitch to create the texture of the acorn cups as shown below.

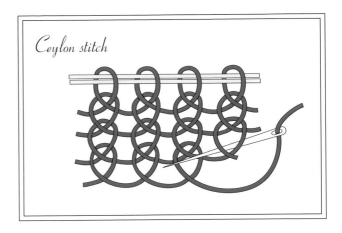

Ceylon stitch

1. Form the top edge of the cup with two satin stitches across the acorn, about halfway down the shape.

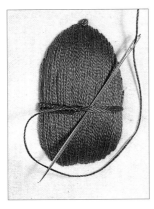

2. Bring the thread up at one side of the acorn, then work a row of slightly-spaced buttonhole stitches over the two satin stitches.

3. Take the thread down behind the acorn shape, bring it back up on the other side slightly below the last row, then work another row of stitches through the loops in the first row.

4. Repeat step 3 until the cup is complete.

The finished embroidery.

27

Poppy Seed Heads

You will need:

Medium-weight calico
Felt
Thin suede
Tracing paper and pencil
Fabric paint and brush
Sewing thread
Six-stranded cotton
No. 7 embroidery needle

Although these poppy seed heads are quite round in appearance, they are not as smooth as the acorns in the previous project. Felt is still used as the padding material, but, here, three layers of felt are sewn on top of each other.

The bulk of each seed head shape is covered with satin stitch (see page 21) and rows of stem stitch (see page 20) create the stalks. The textured top to each seed head is worked on a shaped piece of thin suede and consists of bullion knots worked from the tip of the seed head down to the points of the shape.

Full-size pattern. Use gold fabric paint to transfer all the outlines of this pattern on to the background fabric.

Felt shapes for the long seed head. Cut one set of these shapes.

Felt shapes for the round seed heads. Cut two sets of these shapes.

Layering the felt padding

Layered felt is an ideal method of padding the shapes of these seed heads. Referring to the small diagram (below left), cut out sets of three, different-sized shapes for each seed head.

Then, starting with the smallest shape, use small, neat stab stitches (see page 19) to secure them on top of each other within the gold outlines on the background fabric.

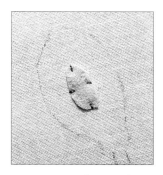

1. Use just four stab stitches to secure the smallest shape in the middle of the outline.

2. Overlay the second layer, secure it initially with four stitches, then stab stitch it all round.

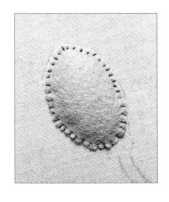

3. Stab stitch the third layer to complete the padding.

4. Work the other two seed head shapes in a similar manner.

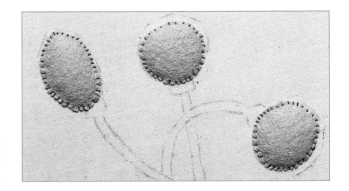

Bullion knot

Bullion knots are long, wrapped stitches, anchored at each end, that can be curled into shapes. The stitch is also known as worm stitch or caterpillar stitch – names which may suggest ideas for using it. Bullion knots can be made in any thickness of thread, but the thread must be smooth.

1. Bring the needle and thread up through the fabric at the top of the shape, insert the needle at one of the points of the shape, then bring it back up through the original hole.

2. Wrap the thread round the needle until the wrapping is long enough for the required stitch.

3. Pull the needle and thread through the wrapping.

4. Fold the wrapping back on itself, then take the thread down through the fabric at the other end of the stitch.

Embroidering the design

Use a No. 7 embroidery needle and one strand of six-stranded cotton to work the stalks on the background fabric; make four or five rows of stem stitch, side by side.

Use long satin stitches to cover the seed heads, working from the top to the bottom of each shape. Work satin stitch across the join between the stalk and the seed head.

Draw the shapes for the tops of the seed heads on to a piece of thin suede. Work six bullion knots on each shape; start each stitch at the top centre of the shape and take it down to one of the points. Trim the shapes to size, then sew them over the top of the seed heads, leaving the bottom of each shape free.

The finished embroidery.

Topiary

In this project, only the short lengths of tree trunk, worked in stem stitch (see page 20), are embroidereded on the background fabric. The circles of foliage are slips, worked entirely in French knots on a separate piece of lightweight calico. These slips need little or no filling, as the surplus calico provides the stuffing. However, a more rounded effect can be achieved by adding toy stuffing.

Petite beads, to represent berries, are sewn on the completed mass of French knot foliage. Air-drying clay was used to make the flowerpot, but you can buy flowerpot buttons.

You will need:

Medium-weight calico
Lightweight calico
Tracing paper and pencil
Fabric paint and brush
Sewing thread
Six-stranded cotton
No. 7 embroidery needle
No. 10 sharps or a
    beading needle
Petite beads
Air-drying clay
Acrylic paint

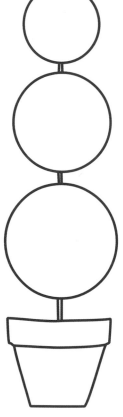

Full-size pattern. Use gold fabric paint to transfer all the outlines of this pattern on to the background fabric.

Making French knot slips

Paint the three circles on a separate piece of lightweight calico, leaving at least 25mm (1in) space between each for cutting out, then fill each circle with a mass of French knots.

French knot

1. Bring the thread up through the fabric, hold the thread taut, then twist the needle round the thread twice.

2. Keeping the thread taut, take the needle back through the fabric just to the side of where the thread comes through it.

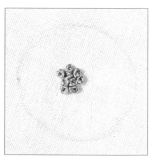

3. Release the thread when the needle has gone through the fabric. Pull the knot tight, then make more knots.

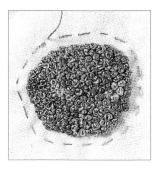   

4. When the shape is full, work small running stitches approximately 6mm (¼in) away from the embroidery. Leave a tail of thread at one end.

5. Cut out the shape, 6mm (¼in) outside the running stitches, then pull the thread to draw the surplus calico up behind the embroidery.

6. Flatten the shape, tucking in the surplus fabric, then secure the loose thread with a couple of stitches. Make the other two slips in the same way.

7. Roll out the clay, cut it into the flowerpot shape, then add a lip along the top edge. Use a pin to make two small holes in the middle of the pot. When the pot is dry, paint it with acrylics and leave it to dry again.

8. Use stab stitches (see page 19) to secure the slips over the painted shapes on the background fabric. Then, using a beading needle and a complementary colour of thread, randomly sew on the fine beads between the French knots.

The finished embroidery. Before sewing the three decorated slips to the background fabric, work the short lengths of the trunk in stem stitch (see page 20). Finally, when the paint is thoroughly dry, sew the flowerpot to the embroidery.

Butterfly

The three-dimensional effects of this butterfly design are all achieved with embroidery stitches; no extra padding is used. The outlines of the butterfly is worked in stem stitch (see page 20). Satin stitch, overlaid with raised stem stitch band creates the body parts. The other decoration is worked with satin stitch (see page 21), padded satin stitch (see page 35), spider's web stitch (see page 34) and a few French knots (see page 30). The coloured diagram shows where these different stitches are used.

You will need:

Medium-weight calico
Tracing paper and pencil
Fabric paint and brush
Six-stranded cotton
No. 7 embroidery needle

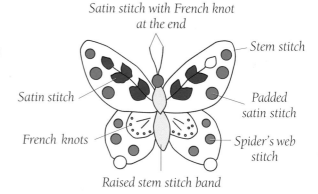

Full-size pattern. Use gold fabric paint to mark all the outlines on to the background fabric.

Stem stitch

Use stem stitch (see page 20) to work the outlines of the wings, the two half circles in the lower wings, the two small circles at the bottom of the wings and all the straight lines.

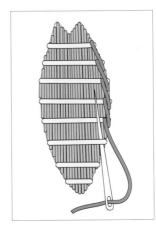
Raised stem stitch band

Work the two parts of the body separately, within each outlined shape. Use complementary colours for the satin stitch base and the straight stitch bars. For clarity, I have used different colours in the diagrams below.

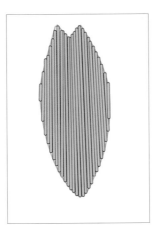

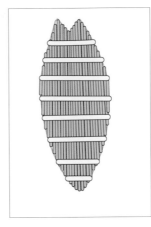

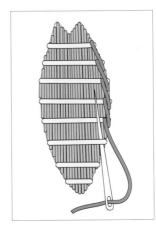

1. Using all six strands of cotton, fill each shape with satin stitches. If you want a more rounded body, sew more layers over the centre section.

2. Next, using one strand of six-stranded cotton, sew a series of spaced straight stitch bars across the body.

3. Finally, work stem stitches over the short straight stitches, making sure you do not pick up the stitches underneath.

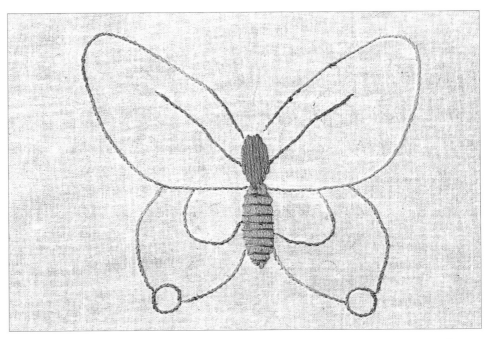

In this photograph, the two halves of the body are at different stages. The top part is complete, while the lower part is ready for the final stem stitches to be applied.

33

Spider's web stitch

This stitch is used to embroider the three small circles in each of the lower wings. I have used contrasting colours in the following diagrams so that the stitches can be seen clearly. For the actual project, use one strand of six-stranded cotton in the same colour or complementary colours.

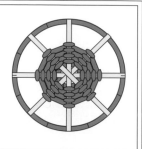

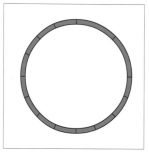
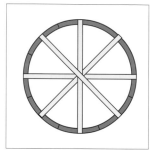

1. Referring to the coloured diagram on page 32, back stitch round the outlines of the shapes to be worked with spider's web stitch.

2. Now, bring the thread up at the edge of the shape, take it across the middle, then down through the opposite edge. Take the thread across the underside of the fabric and bring it back up to the front where you want the next rib to start. Make more ribs in a similar manner.

3. When all the ribs have been made, bring the thread up through the centre of the circle, just to the side of one of the ribs. Take the thread back over and under that rib, then under the next rib. Note that the thread does not pass through the fabric.

4. Take the thread back over and under this rib, then under the next. Continue working round the circle, taking the thread back over one rib then under two, until the desired portion of the circle has been filled. Fasten the thread on the underside of the fabric.

Enlarged view of spider's web stitch in progress.

34

Padded satin stitch

The three circles on each of the upper wings and the butterfly's head are worked with three layers of satin stitch. Each layer is sewn in a different direction on progressively larger circles. Again, for clarity, different colours are used on the diagrams for each layer. For the actual embroidery, use the same or a complementary colour of thread for each layer.

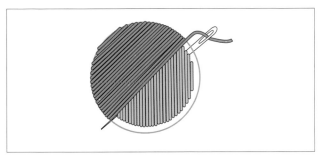

1. First, working an area 3mm (^{1}/$_8$in) inside the drawn circle, fill it with a layer of closely-worked satin stitches (see page 21).

2. Now, working an area 1.5mm (^{1}/$_{16}$in) inside the drawn circle, sew a second layer of closely-worked satin stitches at rightangles to the first.

3. Finally, work a third layer of satin stitches at an angle of about 45° to the previous layer to cover the whole of the drawn area.

Other stitches

The lozenge shapes on the upper wing are worked in satin stitch (see page 21). The antennae are single, long straight stitches with tiny French knots (see page 30) on the end. More French knots complete the design on the lower wings.

This enlarged photograph shows the padded satin stitch circles and the satin stitch lozenge shapes. Note how I have created more interest by varying the direction of the final layer of stitches on each of the padded circles.

The finished embroidery.

NEEDLELACE TECHNIQUES

Needlelace is a technique that is well worth incorporating into stumpwork as it provides lots of textures that cannot be obtained with other embroidery stitches.

Small fragments of lace can be applied to the background fabric or over padded shapes. They can be stiffened with horsehair, to make them stand proud of the surface, or with fine wire to allow them to be bent into freestanding shapes.

Needlelace is worked over a cordonnet (a strong cotton thread laid round the shape to be filled) which is temporarily couched on a needlelace pad with sewing thread. The needlelace pad consists of two or three layers of a backing material, a paper pattern and an overlay to protect the paper pattern from the needle. The filling stitches, which are all variations of detached buttonhole stitch, are all worked with 100/3 silk thread.

In this part of the book, I show you the basic principles of making a simple outline cordonnet (a leaf shape with a centre vein) and how to fill it with two types of filling stitch. I then take you, step by step, through the projects on this sampler, before moving on to more complex designs.

Leaf

Most needlelace shapes have simple outlines, where the cordonnet threads are joined on one side of the shape (see page 44). However, some shapes, such as this leaf with a centre vein, need careful planning to ensure they are able to support the finished needlelace. On these pages, I show you how I make a needlelace pad and how I plan the cordonnet for the leaf. I then show you how to work two basic filling stitches.

You will need:

Medium-weight calico
Paper pattern
Self-adhesive plastic film
No. 7 sharps needle
No. 10 ballpoint needle
Crochet thread No. 80
Sewing thread
100/3 silk thread

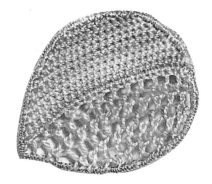

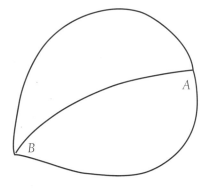

Full-size pattern for the leaf shape.

Needlelace pad

You can make small needlelace pads to suit individual shapes or make them large enough to accommodate several pieces. If you use the latter method, it is best to complete all the shapes on the pad before releasing any of them. Make a sandwich of two or three layers of medium-weight calico, the paper pattern and a transparent, protective overlay.

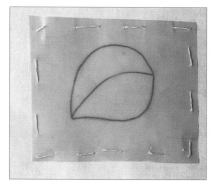

I use architect's linen to protect my paper patterns, but self-adhesive plastic film, which is more readily available, is just as good. Tack all the layers together firmly.

Making a cordonnet

It is essential that cordonnets stay intact when the needlelace is released from the backing fabric, so joins must be kept to a minimum. Take time to plan the layout properly so that you can build a cordonnet from a continuous length of thread. Use the full-size pattern to estimate the length of thread required. Lay the thread along all the lines on the diagram including the central vein, double this length and add a short extra allowance. You will need 380mm (15in) of thread for this leaf.

The following steps show you how to build this particular shape, with its intersections at each end of the centre vein. A more complicated leaf shape, with lots of intersecting veins, is shown on page 73, but it is just an extension of these basic rules.

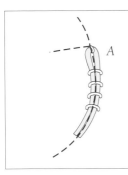

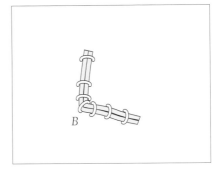

Make the couching stitches small, firm and neat – a poor foundation will result in a disappointing piece of lace. If the couching thread runs out before you have finished the cordonnet, take the thread to the back of the needlelace pad and secure it with three or four stitches, then start a new length.

1. Fold the cordonnet thread roughly in half, making one thread 75mm (3in) longer than the other. Lay the loop end of this thread over point A, then start to couch the cordonnet to the needlelace pad. Bring the sewing thread up from the back of the pad and through the loop of the cordonnet thread, take it over the thread and back down through the same hole. Bring the thread up on the pattern line, 3mm (^{1}/8in) away from point A, make a stitch over both cordonnet threads, then take the sewing thread back through the same hole. Continue round the outline.

2. When you reach point B, make an extra couching stitch at the point of the leaf (a sharp point is useful when making the filling stitches). Continue couching round the outer edge of the leaf back towards point A.

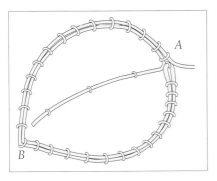

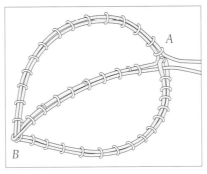

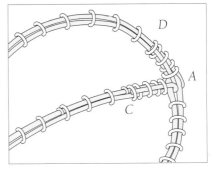

3. When you get back to point A, separate the cordonnet threads. Take the long one towards point B, couching it down in two or three places to hold it in position.

4. At point B, take the thread under and over the couched outline threads, lay it back down against the single thread, pass it through the original loop at point A, then couch down both threads to complete the vein.

6. At point A, fold the thread back on itself, then couch down a short length to point C. Use a large-eyed needle to pull the other thread through the original loop, fold it back to point D, then couch it down. Fasten off the couching thread on the back of the pad, then trim excess threads.

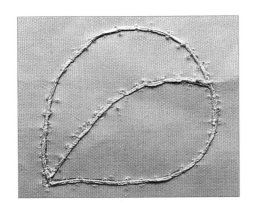

The finished cordonnet.

Filling stitches

One half of the leaf design is filled with single Brussels stitch, the other with corded single Brussels stitch. Both halves are worked from the central vein out to the edges. The filling stitches do not pass through the sandwiched layers of the needlelace pad, but are worked over and supported on the cordonnet threads.

Joins in the filling stitches can only be made at the end of each row, so you must ensure that you always have sufficient thread to work a full row of stitches. A good guide is to have at least three to four times the length of the space being worked.

Single Brussels stitch

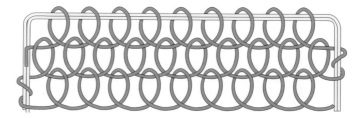

Start this stitch with a row of buttonhole stitches across the cordonnet. The spacing of this foundation row of stitches governs the texture of the finished piece: use loose stitches for an open texture; tight ones for a dense texture. Subsequent rows of stitches are looped into those above.

Corded single Brussels stitch

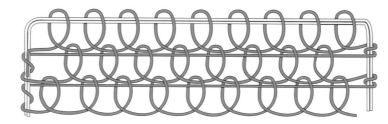

This stitch is worked in much the same way as that above except that, at the end of each row of buttonhole stitches, the thread is laid back across the work as a 'cord', then the next row of stitches is worked round this cord and the loops in the previous row.

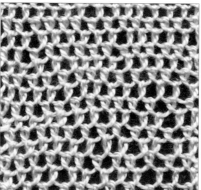

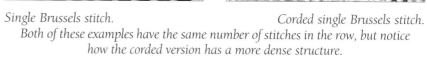

Single Brussels stitch.   Corded single Brussels stitch.
Both of these examples have the same number of stitches in the row, but notice how the corded version has a more dense structure.

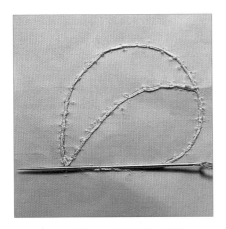 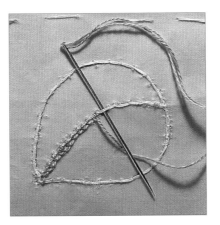 

1. Secure the end of the filling stitch thread to the cordonnet by passing it under a few of the couching stitches. Take it through to a point just short of the intersection between the centre vein and the outline of the leaf.

2. Work a row of evenly-spaced buttonhole stitches across the central vein of the cordonnet. Do not pull the stitches too tight as you must work through their loops for the next row.

This enlarged view of the first row of buttonhole stitches shows how the loops are formed as you progress.

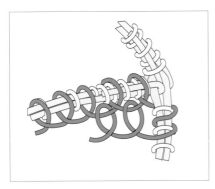

3. When you reach the end of the row attach the thread to the side of the cordonnet. Take the needle and thread under both cordonnet threads, then whip it over **both** threads – allowing for the depth of the stitches – down to the point where you want to start the next row.

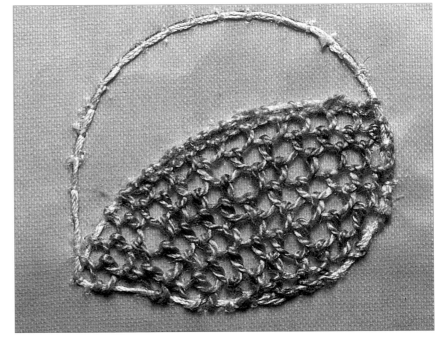

4. Work back across the shape, working one buttonhole stitch in each loop of the previous row. Whip the thread round the cordonnet again then work back across the shape. Continue until the area is filled. Always take your needle and thread straight out under the cordonnet threads, this will help to keep the rows straight. Secure the last row of stitches by whipping each loop to the cordonnet.

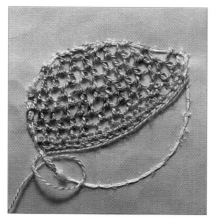

5. Turn the leaf shape round, attach another silk thread to the cordonnet, then work a row of buttonhole stitches, slightly tighter than those in step 2, across the centre vein. At the end of the row, take the thread under, over and under the cordonnet.

6. Lay the thread back across the space, just under the loops of the first row to form the cord. At the left-hand edge of the design whip the thread down the cordonnet to the start point for the next row of stitches.

7. Work another row of buttonhole stitches; this time, work the stitches into each loop of the previous row and under the laid cord.

8. Repeat steps 6 and 7 until the whole area is filled, then whip the last row of loops to the cordonnet as in step 4.

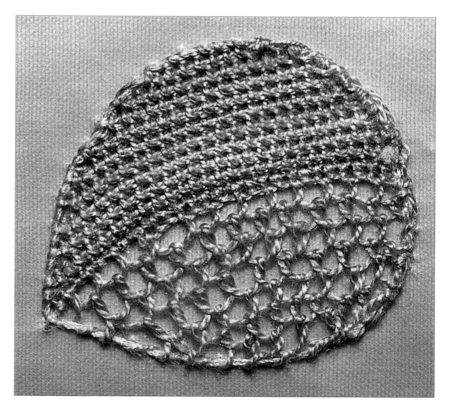

Top stitching and releasing the needlelace

One characteristic of needlelace is a raised outer edge. This is made by laying two threads over the cordonnet, then covering these and the cordonnet threads with a row of buttonhole stitches. Work the buttonhole stitches as close together as possible, preferably with the loops lying towards the outer edge of the shape. When the top stitching is complete, the needlelace is released from the fabric backing and assembled on the embroidery.

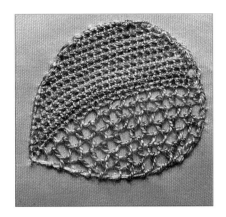

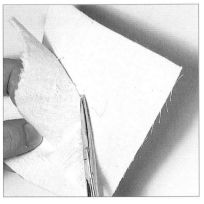

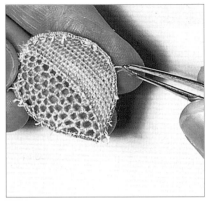

1. Cut another length of cordonnet thread long enough to go twice around the shape, with a little extra for good measure (see page 38). Fold it in half, then use the silk thread to whip the loop end to the existing cordonnet threads. Now, using the silk thread, work tight buttonhole stitches all round the shape.

2. Remove the tacking stitches around the design, fold back the bottom layer of calico, then use fine-pointed scissors to snip through all the couching stitches.

3. Remove the needlelace, then use a pair of tweezers to remove any remaining fragments of the couching threads from the back of the lace.

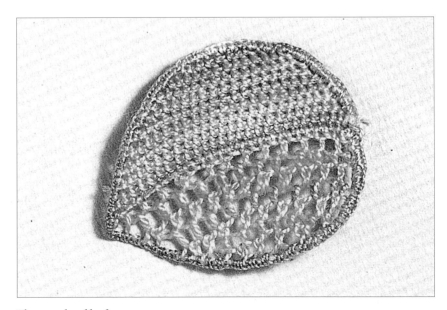

The completed leaf.

Flower

For this first needlelace project, I have chosen a simple flower design. The flower bud is raised on padded felt (see page 26). The stalks are paper-covered wire which is wrapped with silk thread, then couched on the background fabric. The needlelace shapes are filled with single and corded single Brussels stitch (see pages 40–42), and double Brussels stitch. The freestanding petals are only secured at the centre of the flower. The base is a calico slip, covered with French knots.

You will need:

Needlelace pads (see page 38)
Crochet thread No. 80
Sewing thread
Lightweight calico for the slip
   and finished embroidery
Fabric paint and brushes
No. 9 sharps needle
Two No. 10 ballpoint needles
100/3 silk thread
Felt
Toy stuffing
Paper-covered wire

Cordonnet diagrams for petals and the parts of the bud.

A

Enlarged view of the cordonnet for the flower petals. Make the join at point A.

Full-size pattern. The flower petals are freestanding, so use gold fabric paint to transfer just the three long stalks, the leaf and its stalk, the bud shape and the centres of the two flowers on to the base fabric.

Cordonnets

Referring to page 38, make needlelace pads for all the needlelace shapes. Use the small diagrams for all the petals and the bud, and the full-size pattern for the leaf shape (please note that this is not exactly the same shape as the leaf shape on page 38).

Transfer the shape of the base on to a piece of lightweight calico in preparation for a slip.

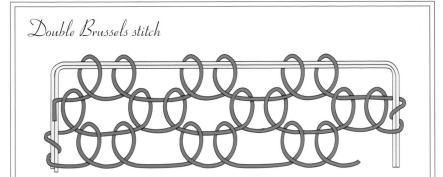

Double Brussels stitch

This is similar to single Brussels stitch, except that the first row of buttonhole stitches consists of spaced pairs of stitches – the space between each pair being the width of a pair of stitches. On subsequent rows, pairs of stitches are worked over the loops between the pairs of stitches in the row above.

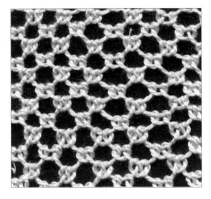

Double Brussels stitch.

Needlelace petals

Referring to the general instructions on page 38 and the cordonnet diagram, build cordonnets for each petal. Start at point A, take the doubled thread round the shape, pass both threads through the loop, turn them back and couch down the ends.

Make five petal shapes filled with single Brussels stitch (see page 40) and ten more filled with double Brussels stitch (see above). Top stitch round the outside of each petal as detailed on page 43.

Needlelace bud

The cordonnets for the bud parts are laid in a similar way to the petals, then each shape is filled with corded single Brussels stitch (see page 40). Do not top stitch round these shapes.

Needlelace leaf

For this project, the leaf includes a turned-over section which is worked over the top of the basic leaf shape before top stitching it. When filling curved shapes with corded needlelace, you will have more control over the cord by working with two needles.

Make a cordonnet for the leaf similar to that on page 39, then fill one half with single Brussels stitch and the other with corded single Brussels stitch (see

pages 40). Do not top stitch the shape yet. Work the turned-over shape with two needles and two lengths of thread as described below – for clarity, I have shown the two threads in different colours.

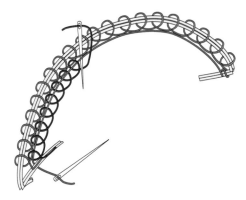

Attach the first thread (shown in green) to the centre vein of the cordonnet, then make a row of buttonhole stitches along the outer edge of the leaf, over the previously worked needlelace. Whip the thread round the right-hand end of the cordonnet, then lay the thread back across the shape and take it under the left-hand end of the cordonnet. Do not secure this thread.

Attach the other thread (shown in pink) to the cordonnet, then start to work a second row of buttonhole stitches into the loops of the previous row and over the loose-laid cord.

When you reach the end of the second row, whip the thread round the left-hand end of the cordonnet, then lay the thread back across the row and under the right-hand end of the cordonnet. Do not secure this thread. Pick up the first needle and thread, whip it round the cordonnet, then start to work the third row of stitches.

Finish the third row of stitches, whip the thread round the right-hand end, then lay the thread back. Make a fourth row of stitches with the other thread, then, instead of laying a cord, whip the thread back across the shape, working into each loop of the last row of stitches. Fasten off both threads into the cordonnet. Top stitch round the outer edge of the whole leaf shape and along the centre vein, then release from the pad as shown on page 43. Do not top stitch round the loose edge of the turnover section.

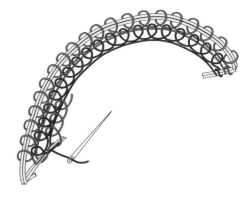

Finishing the embroidery

When all the needlelace parts of the design have been made, the embroidery can be assembled.

1. Measure the lengths of the three flower stalks and the leaf stalk, then cut a length of paper-covered wire for each. Dip one end of a wire into white glue, then, starting 25mm (1in) from the tip, loosely wrap silk thread back towards the tip. At the tip, pinch the thread into the glue, then wrap the thread as closely as possible down the length of the wire. Secure the end of the thread with a touch more glue. Couch all four stalks over the out-lines on the background fabric (see page 23).

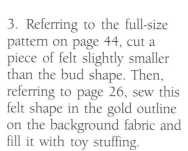

2. Make the short twisted stalk by winding a wrapped stem around a fine knitting needle or a large bodkin needle. Couch this on to the background fabric.

3. Referring to the full-size pattern on page 44, cut a piece of felt slightly smaller than the bud shape. Then, referring to page 26, sew this felt shape in the gold outline on the background fabric and fill it with toy stuffing.

Sew the needlelace bud pieces over the felt pad.

4. Sew the small sides of five of the double Brussels stitch petals round the gold outline of each flower centre. Overlap the petals slightly to make them look natural.

5. Sew the five single Brussels stitch petals over the double Brussels stitch petals on the top flower head.

6. Make the centres for the flowers. Cut a 20cm (8in) length of yellow thread. Thread one end of this into a needle, then wrap 15cm (6in) of the other end round a pencil. Carefully slip the wrapping from the pencil, catch the loops together with the needle and thread, then sew the loop securely in the middle of a flower head. Cut the loops and fray the ends out to resemble stamens.

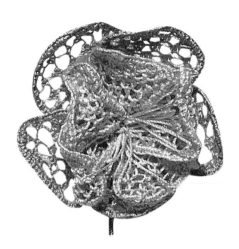

7. Sew the leaf over the end of its stalk.

The finished embroidery.

8. Use the base shape (see pattern on page 44) to make a small slip filled with French Knots. Sew this over the bottom of the stalks.

Seaweed and Fish

In this project, all the needlelace shapes are worked in corded single Brussels stitch (see page 40). The edges of the seaweed shapes are wired before they are top stitched to allow them to be entwined and stand free. The two striped fish, which are worked in two colours, are applied over layered felt (see page 28). The two rocks are slips made from painted lightweight calico stretched over pieces of interfacing.

You will need:

Needlelace pads (see page 38)
Crochet thread No. 80
Sewing thread
Lightweight calico for the slip
   and the finished embroidery
Fabric paint and brushes
No. 9 sharps needle
No. 10 ballpoint needle
100/3 silk thread
Felt
Petite bead
Fine wire
Interfacing (or card)

Full size pattern. The bracts of seaweed are freestanding so use gold fabric paint to mark just the outlines of the two fish and the two rocks on to the background fabric.

Cordonnets

Use the exploded diagram to make cordonnets for the four bracts of seaweed and the two fish. Remember to make the joins on one of the long edges of each shape.

Full-size pattern for making cordonnets and slips.

Changing colours

This diagram shows single corded Brussels stitch, but the same method of changing colour works with any filling stitch.

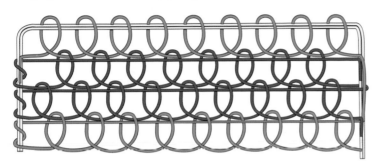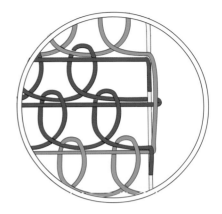

Join the first colour thread to one side of the cordonnet, then work filling stitches down to the point where you want to change colour. At the end of this row of buttonhole stitches, leave the thread to one side (do not lay the thread back across the row).

Join the new colour to the cordonnet, lay it as a cord across the shape, whip it down the other side, then work filling stitches in this colour until you want to change colour once more. If you intend using the second colour again, leave it to one side. Otherwise, run it through the couching stitches on the cordonnet and trim off the excess thread. Run the first colour thread down through the couching stitches on the cordonnet to a point level with the bottom of the last row of stitches, lay in a cord, then work filling stitches in the rest of the shape or until you want to change colour again.

Needlelace fish

The two striped fish are worked with two needles threaded with different colours as shown in the diagram above. The petite bead used for the fish's eye is threaded on to one of the laid cords, then the next row of filling stitches is worked around the bead at the required position. Alternatively, you could make the eye with a small French knot. Do not top stitch round the fish shapes, as they are applied to padded shapes on the background fabric.

Needlelace seaweed

Fill all the shapes with corded single Brussels stitch. Loosely whip a length of fine wire round each shape, then top stitch and release each shape (see page 43). Reinforcing the edges of these shapes with fine wire, instead of the usual two threads, make the bracts stiffer and easier to mould into shape.

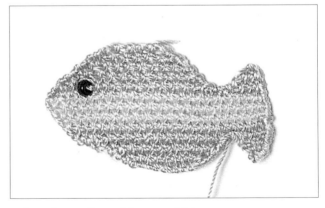

Enlarged view of one of the striped fish.

Finishing the embroidery

1. Sew the bottom edges of the seaweed bracts on to the background fabric, overlapping them so that their fronds can be entwined. Most of the left-hand side of the long stem of seaweed shape 3 (see page 48) and the right-hand side of the long stem on shape 4 are also sewn to the background fabric, leaving just their top ends free.

2. Referring to the pattern on page 48 and the layered felt instructions on page 28, cut three layers of felt for each fish shape. Make the largest shape slightly smaller than the pattern, and omit the shape of the tails on all layers. Working from the smallest shape upwards, stab stitch each one to the background fabric, overlapping the sewn-down parts of the seaweed.

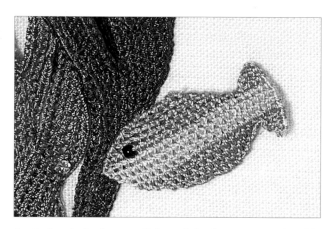

3. Stab stitch the needlelace fish shapes over the felt pads; secure just their bodies, leaving their tails free to give the impression that they are swimming.

The finished embroidery.

4. The rock shapes are slips of lightweight calico, painted with pearlised colour to give the rocks a textured appearance. The painted area of calico should be large enough to cut out oversize shapes with an allowance of 6mm (¼in) all round. When the paint is thoroughly dry, decorate the shape with embroidery detail (if required), then cut them out.

Cut full-size rock shapes from a piece of interfacing (or cardboard if you want stiffer rocks). Stretch the calico over the interfacing shape and lightly glue the turned-over edges to the back of the interfacing. Stab stitch the bottom edges of the rocks over the base of the seaweed.

50

The inspiration for this picture came from a visit to a marine aquatic centre. The seahorse seemed to be motionless and oblivious to the hustle and bustle of the brightly coloured fish around him.

The seahorse is worked in needlelace over a stuffed felt pad. The fish are calico-covered interfacing slips, embroidered with satin stitch. The seaweed is cut from two layers of painted silk bonded together with iron-on interfacing (see page 75). The pattern for the seahorse is shown on page 78.

Orange Branch

This design includes five realistic oranges which are made by covering cotton moulds with single Brussels stitch. The leaves are made in much the same way as those shown previously, using both single and double Brussels stitch. However, three of the leaves are worked on the background fabric of the finished embroidery, using a cordonnet of back stitches.

You will need:

Needlelace pads (see page 38)
Crochet thread No. 80
Sewing thread
Lightweight calico for the
    finished embroidery
Fabric paint and brushes
Cotton moulds
No. 9 sharps needle
No. 10 ballpoint needle
100/3 silk thread
Six-stranded cotton
Fine wire
Horsehair
Stiletto

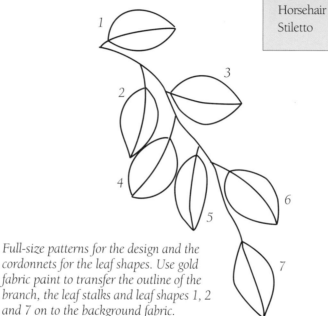

Full-size patterns for the design and the cordonnets for the leaf shapes. Use gold fabric paint to transfer the outline of the branch, the leaf stalks and leaf shapes 1, 2 and 7 on to the background fabric.

Back stitch

Cordonnets

Use the full-size patterns to make cordonnets for leaf shapes 3, 4, 5, and 6, as described on pages 38–39. Work the cordonnets of leaf shapes 1, 2 and 7 on the background fabric by back stitching round the gold outline of each shape.

Needlelace oranges

The oranges are cotton moulds covered with needlelace. Unlike the other leaf shapes and the stalks, which are worked with silk thread, these are worked with one strand of six-stranded cotton.

I always paint cotton moulds to match the colour of the thread used to cover them. This is not essential, but a painted mould does mask any irregularities in the needlelace. However, for clarity, I worked these step-by-step photographs on a plain, white cotton mould.

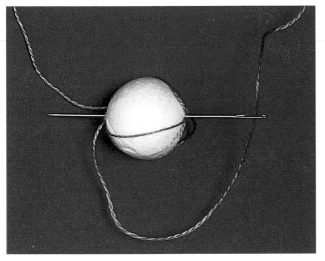

1. Using a No. 9 embroidery needle, take a long length of cotton thread down through the centre of the mould, bring the thread up round the outside of the mould, then back down through the centre to form a vertical stitch round the mould. Continue until you have made approximately ten stitches.

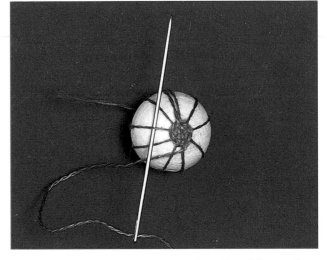

2. Cut a new length of cotton thread and bring the thread up through to the top of the cotton mould. Weave this thread through the vertical stitches, taking it round two or three times.

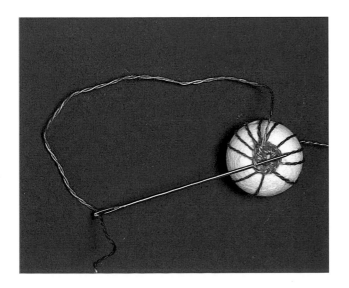

3. Now, using the same length of thread, start to work tiny single Brussels stitches, as close together as possible, over the last row of woven threads. You can disregard the vertical stitches, which have now served their purpose.

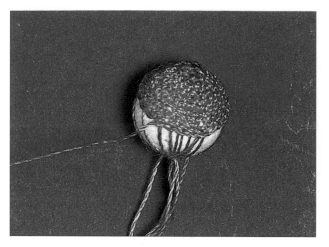

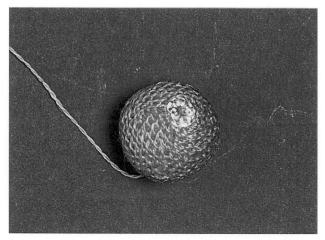

4. Continue the filling stitches round the mould, working them into the loops of the stitches immediately above. As the shape gets bigger, increase the number of stitches by working two loops into one. When the thread starts to run out, take the short end down, round the outside of the mould, to the bottom and anchor it under two or three of the vertical stitches. Attach a new length of thread under the same vertical stitches, bring it up to the needlelace and link it through the last completed loop, then continue working the filling stitches.

5. When you pass the widest part of the mould, decrease the stitches by missing out some of the loops in the previous row. When the whole mould is covered, trim off the excess lengths of all bar one of the loose threads. Use a cocktail stick to apply a spot of glue to the underside of the cotton mould, then push all the trimmed lengths into the recess. Finally, using one strand of green cotton thread, work a few rows of buttonhole stitches over the orange ones.

Needlelace leaves

Make leaf shapes 3, 4, 5 and 6 in needlelace, using your choice of filling stitches. Before top stitching them, lay one strand of horsehair round leaf shapes 4 and 6, and one strand of fine wire round leaf shapes 3 and 5. Leave tails of horsehair and fine wire at the base of each leaf shape to attach the shapes to the background fabric.

Fill leaf shapes 1, 2 and 7 with your choice of filling stitches, within the back-stitched cordonnets on the background fabric. Do not top stitch round these shapes.

Finishing the embroidery

Work the branch and the short leaf stalks in stem stitch. Decide on the arrangement of the freestanding leaves and oranges. Use a stiletto to make small holes in the background fabric at the appropriate places, take the wire and horsehair tails on the leaves, and the cotton thread on the oranges through to the back of the work, then secure them with a few oversewn stitches. Finally, shape the freestanding leaves.

The finished embroidery.

54

This design is typical of 17th Century stumpwork in that the fruit and leaves are completely out of scale to the size of the tree. It is made entirely of needlelace shapes, worked in much the same way as the previous project. I used eight different types of filling stitch for the base.

Mushrooms

All the elements of this design are needlelace shapes except for the four small patches of grass at the base of each mushroom which are slips filled with French knots. All the padding is stuffed felt. The pads for the mushroom stalks are prepared in exactly the same way as in previous projects (see page 26), but the pads for the mushroom caps are left open along their bottom edges. The layered structure of the mushrooms means that the needlelace elements must be layered, with some pads sewn on top of needlelace shapes. I introduce a new filling stitch, crossbar stitch, and I decorate the tops of some of the mushrooms with buttonholed loops.

You will need:
Needlelace pads (see page 38)
Crochet thread No. 80
Fabric paint and brush
Sewing thread
Lightweight calico for the slips
    and finished embroidery
No. 9 sharps needle
No. 10 ballpoint needle
100/3 silk thread
Felt
Toy stuffing

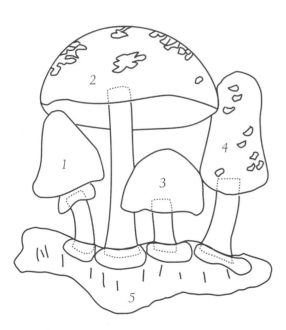

Full-size pattern. Use gold fabric paint to outline the shapes of the mushroom heads, their stalks and the large grass base on to the background fabric. The dotted lines at the top and bottom of the stalks show the size of the shapes for the felt pads.

Exploded diagram showing the full-size shapes for the cordonnets and slips.

56

Cordonnets

Use the exploded diagram to make cordonnets for all shapes, except shapes 6a–6d, which are slips.

Slips

Prepare French knot slips for the four grass shapes 6a–6d (see page 30).

Enlarged view of crossbar stitch.

Crossbar stitch

This is a variation of Double Brussels stitch (see page 45). Make a foundation row of spaced pairs of stitches – the space between each pair being the width of a pair of stitches – then make a second row of stitches, looping each stitch into the stitch above. On the next row, make two stitches into the loops between the pairs of stitches in the previous row, then make another row of stitches, looping each stitch into the stitch above. Repeat until the shape is filled.

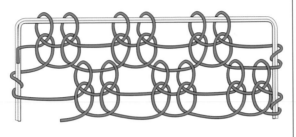

Needlelace shapes

Work the stalk shapes 1c, 2c, 3b and 4b, the mushroom cap shapes 2a, 2b, 1b and 4a, and the grass base shape 5 in corded single Brussels stitch.

Work the mushroom cap shape 1a in corded double Brussels stitch. Work the mushroom cap shape 3a in crossbar stitch.

Top stitch along just the bottom sections of cap shapes 1a, 1b, 2b, 3a and 4a. The cap shape 2a, the stalk shape 1c, 2c, 3b and 4b, and the grass shape 5 do not require top stitching as they are sewn to the background fabric.

Enlarged view of the needlelace shape 1a which is worked in corded double Brussels stitch, and shape 3a which is worked in crossbar stitch. Notice that base shapes are top stitched across the bottom edges.

Finishing the embroidery

1. Sew the needlelace grass shape 5 to the background fabric.

2. Referring to the full-size pattern on page 56, cut slightly undersize pieces of felt for the stalk shapes of all four mushrooms.

3. Stab stitch the felt shapes for mushrooms 1, 3 and 4 to the grass base and the background fabric, then fill them with toy stuffing (see page 26).

4. Apply the needlelace stalk shapes 1c, 3b and 4b over the felt pads.

5. Apply the ring shape 1b over its stalk. Sew just the sides and top to the background fabric, leaving the bottom edge free.

6. Cut a slightly undersize piece of felt for the cap of mushroom 4, then secure its sides and top edges to the background fabric. Fill the shape with toy stuffing,

then, as the bottom of the felt shape is left open, secure the stuffing with three or four loose stab stitches approximately 6mm (¼in) up from the bottom of the felt. Take these stab stitches through to the back of the background fabric, but do not pull them tight. Apply the needlelace shape 4a over its felt pad, leaving the bottom edge free.

7. Sew the needlelace cap shape 2a to the background fabric and over the edge of mushroom cap shape 4a.

8. Stab stitch the felt stalk shape for mushroom 2 to the background fabric and over the bottom needlelace section of its cap, then fill it with toy stuffing. Sew the needlelace stalk shape 2c to its pad.

9. Referring to step 6, cut, apply and fill a piece of felt for the top section of the cap of mushroom 2, then apply the needlelace shape 2b over the felt pad. Remember to leave its bottom edge free.

10. Cut and apply a piece of felt for the cap of mushroom 1, laying a small section of this over the bottom part of the cap of mushroom 2. Fill the felt with toy stuffing, then apply the needlelace shape 1a over the felt pad.

11. Repeat step 10 for the cap of mushroom 3: a small part of this fits over the stalk of mushroom 2.

The finished embroidery.

Buttonholed Loops

Knot a silk thread, bring the needle up at point A, then back down through the work at point B – approximately 5mm (¼in) away – leaving a small loop. Repeat this stitch to make a three-stranded loop on the surface. Bring the thread back up at point A, then make a series of close buttonhole stitches over the loop. At the end of the loop, take the thread to the back of the work just above point B. Gently pull the thread to make the stitched loop twist up off the surface, then fasten off.

12. Referring to the diagram and instructions above, decorate the caps of mushrooms 2 and 4 by overstitching them with groups of five or seven buttonholed loops, sewn through all layers.

13. Apply the four French-knot slips over the bottom of the mushroom stalks, sewing them along just the bottom edges.

14. Finally, make some small tufts of grass in the same way as the stamens for the flower heads on page 47, then sew these to the grass base.

Foxgloves

This design, with its tubular, bell-shaped flowers, introduces the use of a wooden embroidery shoe to make the needlelace shapes for the flower heads. Six of the flower heads are worked on normal needlelace pads, four are worked straight on cordonnets back stitched on the background fabric. All the needlelace pieces are filled with corded single Brussels stitch, then decorated with groups of French knots. The flower stalk is a slip of silk fabric stretched over a single layer of felt.

You will need:

Needlelace pads (see page 38)
Crochet thread No. 80
Sewing thread
Lightweight calico for the
    finished embroidery
Fabric paint and brushes
No. 9 sharps needle
No. 10 ballpoint needle
100/3 silk thread
Wooden embroidery shoe
Silk fabric
Felt
Toy stuffing
PVA glue

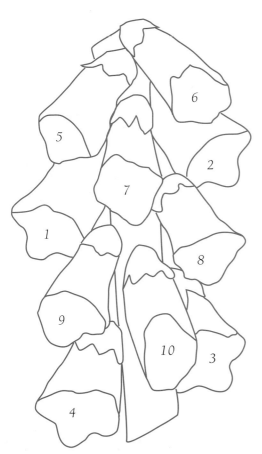

Full-size pattern. Use gold fabric paint to outline the flower stalk and flower head shapes 1–4 on to the background fabric.

Cordonnet diagrams for the caps and flower heads.

Cordonnets

Use the small diagrams above to prepare cordonnets for the flower heads and caps. Six of the flowers are worked on needlelace pads; four are worked on the background fabric (see page 52). You only need to make eight caps, as the tops of flowers 1 and 2 are completely covered by other parts of the embroidery.

Each flower head consists of two layers of needlelace, so it is essential that the couching stitches used for the cordonnets that are made on needlelace pads are firm and close together. Use short back stitches to make the cordonnets for the flower heads 1–4 on the background fabric.

Needlelace flowers

Foxgloves are tubular in shape, and two layers of needlelace must be worked on the same cordonnet to make the shape. A wooden embroidery shoe keeps the top and bottom layers separate and helps to create a more rounded shape. Corded single Brussels stitch (see page 40) is used to fill both layers, but a slight variation is introduced on the last rows of the top piece to create a flared edge.

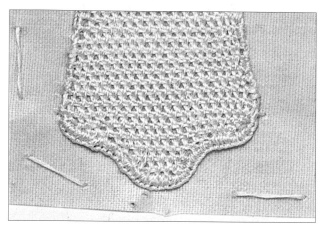

1. Make the bottom half of the eight loose flower-heads on needlelace pads, filling the shape with corded single Brussels stitch.

2. Go back to the top of the cordonnet, then work five rows of corded single Brussels stitch over the bottom layer of needlelace.

3. Place the wooden embroidery shoe under the five rows of the top layer and secure it in position with three or four oversewing stitches on the neck of the shoe.

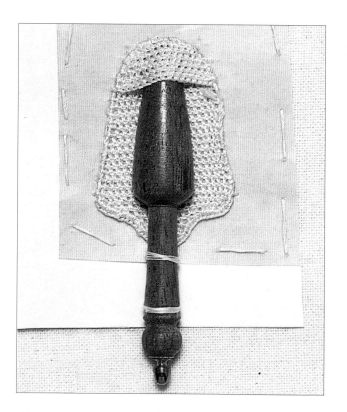

4. Continue down the shape, working rows of stitches over the shoe until you are ready to finish the shape. Refer to the full-size pattern to determine the depth of each top layer.

5. At the end of a row of stitches, do not lay a cord across the shape. Instead, work back across the row making two stitches into the first loop of the previous row, one stitch into the next loop, two stitches into the next loop, etc.

6. Repeat step 5, lay a cord across the shape, top stitch over the cord and through each loop of the last row of filling stitches, then remove the flower and shoe from the backing pad.

7. Dab a few spots of PVA glue on a small amount of toy stuffing, then insert the stuffing between the two layers of needlelace to create a tubular shape.

8. Referring to the finished embroidery, decorate the flower head with a random group of French knots sewn into the bottom layer of needlelace

9. Repeat steps 1–8 for the flower head shapes 1, 2, 3 and 4, over the back-stitched cordonnets on the background fabric.

Needlelace caps

Work eight caps for the foxgloves (flower head shapes 1 and 2 do not require these), top stitch all round each shape, then remove them from the backing pad.

Slip

Referring to the full-size pattern, cut a piece of felt to fit the shape of the stalk. Cut a piece of silk fabric, allowing for a 6mm (¼in) turnover on each edge. Secure the turnovers to the back of the felt with a few spots of PVA.

Finishing the embroidery

1. Sew the flower-stalk slip to the background fabric, laying it over flower head shapes 1–4.

2. Sew the top ends of flower head shapes 5–10 to the stalk and background fabric.

3. Finally, sew the needlelace caps to the top of the flower heads, leaving the bottom edges free.

The finished embroidery.

SCENES AND FIGURES

Here, I show you how to use embroidery, needlelace and other techniques to create embroidered scenes. I also show you how I make heads and hands so that you can add figures into a scene.

Birds and Beach

This delightful beach scene was inspired by some sketches I made while on holiday. The painted background adds a touch of realism to this type of embroidery. All the needlelace shapes are filled with single and corded single Brussels stitches. Satin stitch is used to cover some of the rocks and to define the birds' legs and beaks, and French knots form the birds' eyes. I also introduce a new technique – ruching tubular ribbon over lengths of double knitting wool – to create the waves.

Enlarge this diagram by 150% to make a full-size pattern. When the background washes have been fixed, use gold fabric paint to outline the birds shapes B1–B4, all the rocks and the two posts on to the background fabric.

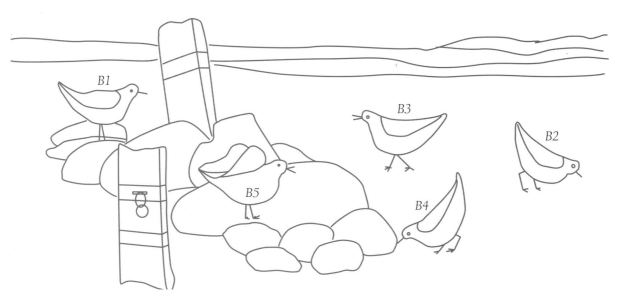

Painting the background

Dampen the top half of the background fabric with clean water, then lay in a wash of pale blue for the sky. Dampen the bottom half of the background fabric, leaving a small dry gap under the sky colour, then apply a wash of golden sand colour. Leave the fabric to dry completely, then iron it to set the paint. Use gold fabric paint to outline the shapes for birds B1–B4, the rocks and the two posts on the background fabric.

Waves

Using a pale blue silk thread, work a row of small back stitches (see page 52) right across the horizon.

Ruche a 150mm (6in) length of tubular ribbon on a 100mm (4in) length of double knitting wool, then pin each end of the ribbon just above the right-hand side of the back-stitched horizon.

Starting at the left-hand side, work a row of single Brussels stitch into the back stitches. When you reach the ruched ribbon, enclose the end of the wool, then work spaced stitches over the length of the ribbon, attaching it to the back stitches.

Ruche a 175mm (7in) length of ribbon on a 125mm (5in) length of wool, then pin this at the right-hand side, just under the last row of stitches. Ruche a 125mm (5in) length of ribbon on a 75mm (3in) length of wool, then pin this at the left-hand side. Work a row of single Brussels stitch, from right to left, enclosing the ends of the wool and attaching the lengths of ribbon to the previous row of stitches.

Work another full row of single Brussels stitch, from left to right. Ruche a 150mm (6in) length of tubular ribbon on a 100mm (4in) length of double knitting wool, then pin over the right-hand side of the last row of needlelace. Work another row of single Brussels stitch, from right to left, enclosing the ends of the wool and attaching the lengths of ribbon to the previous row of stitches. Complete the sea by working a few short rows of single Brussels stitch.

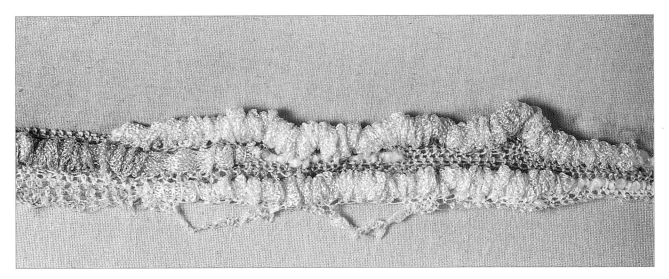

Close-up of the right-hand side of the waves.

Posts

Paint the rough side of a 200mm (8in) square of iron-on interfacing brown, then leave this to dry overnight. Turn the painted surface face down on a piece of lightweight calico, bond the two together with an iron, remove the backing paper, then leave the calico to dry. Cut and fold pieces of card to create two boxes, each 50 x 20 x 6mm (2 x ¾ x ¼in). Use a craft knife to shape the ends of each box. Cut a 6 x 150mm (¼ x 6in) strip of copper sheet, rub shoe polish on the surface to create the appearance of 'rusty metal', then cut it into three 50mm (2in) strips.

Cut two 65 x 50mm (2½ x 2in) pieces of the painted interfaced calico, then glue one piece on each box, tucking the excess into the top end. Glue and wrap one copper strip round one post and two round the other. Working carefully, sew the rear post in position (the front one is attached later).

Rocks

Use the exploded diagram to make pieces of needlelace for rock shapes 3, 5 and 7.

Use fabric paint to colour a 125mm (5in) square piece of interfacing, then, when the paint is dry, cut out full-size shapes for rocks 1, 2, 4, 6 and 8–12. Use gold fabric paint to draw the shapes of these same rocks on a piece of lightweight calico, allowing 20mm (¾in) round each shape for cutting out. Use a variety of threads to cover each shape with satin stitch (see page 21), then cut them out allowing for turnovers. Stretch each piece of calico over its corresponding piece of interfacing, then lightly glue the turned-over edges to the back of the interfacing.

Stab stitch the bottom edges of rock shape slips 1, 2 and 6 to the background fabric. Referring to page 28, cut three layers of felt for rocks 3, 5 and 7. Apply felt for rock 3 so that it slightly overlaps rock slip 2, then cover it with the corresponding needlelace shape. Stab stitch rock slip 4 to the background fabric, then apply the felt layers and needlelace shapes for rocks 5 and 7. Stab stitch the slips for the remaining rocks.

Carefully sew the front post to the background fabric and rock 4. Cut small pebble shapes from the remains of the painted interfacing, then stab stitch these along the bottom edge of the rocks. Sew small beads between these pebbles.

Close-up of bird B5, standing on the needlelace rock.

Birds

Use the exploded diagram to make needlelace pieces (corded single Brussels stitch) for the wing and body shapes for the birds. Bird B5 is double-sided and has two wings, so make extra pieces for this bird.

Cut slightly undersize pieces of felt for birds B1–B4, sew these in position on the background fabric, then fill them with toy stuffing. Sew the needlelace body shapes over the corresponding felt pads, then apply the wings. Use satin stitch to define the legs, feet and beaks and a small French knot for each eye.

Sew the two body shapes for bird B5 together with small stab stitches, then fill it with toy stuffing. Wrap two very short lengths of wire for the legs and two more for the beak. Apply a dab of PVA to the ends of the legs, then push one end into the padded body and the other into the padded rock. Glue the end of the beak wires then push these, slightly apart, into the head.

Finally, work a few horizontal satin stitches across the beach, around each bird and in front of the rocks to denote rivulets of water.

The finished embroidery.

Heads and Hands

Including figures in your designs will increase the range of subjects you can cover. However, such figures must look real, especially with regard to the most visible body shapes – heads and hands – and on these pages, I show you how I go about making realistic figures.

Heads

I always make a complete head as a slip, then, if I am unhappy with the result, I can easily make another. If you sew the padded head shape (as at step 3) to the background fabric, then decorate it, it may prove very difficult to remove it from the background fabric if you do not like the finished face.

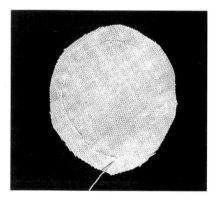

1. Cut a piece of lightweight calico (on the cross of the fabric), 6mm (¼in) larger than the size of the face you want to make. Knot the end of a length of sewing thread, then, starting at the bottom of the shape, make a running stitch just inside the edge of the calico. Leave the thread loose at the bottom of the shape.

2. Pull the loose thread to draw in the edges of the calico and create an open pouch until you have the size of face you want.

3. Use a cocktail stick to help fill the pouch with toy stuffing.

Chain stitch

4. Turn the head shape over and stitch it on another piece of lightweight calico mounted in a hoop. Starting at the chin, sew about three-quarters of the way up each side of the face, add more stuffing to make the head quite firm, then finish sewing round the shape.

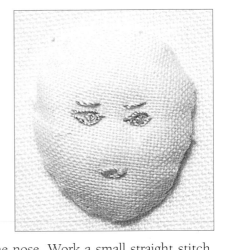

5. Determine the positions for the eyes and mouth; make a very small pencil mark or a small back stitch in the correct positions. Eyes should be on a horizontal line, one-third of the way down the face. The mouth should be one-third of the way up the face. Use fine threads, slightly darker than the calico, to complete the facial features.

Work each eye in chain stitch, starting at the outer edge across to the nose. Pull the thread down quite tightly to form a bridge for the nose. Work a small straight stitch across the bottom of the eye to open it. Make a small French knot for the pupils. Work more small straight stitches for the eyebrows.

Make another chain stitch for the mouth, and open this if necessary with a small straight stitch across the bottom edge.

6. Decide on shapes for the hairstyle, then cut two small pieces of felt to suit. Sew these round the top of the head, then make two or three stitches to secure the felt to the face (do not pull these stitches too tightly).

7. Use long satin stitches to embroider the hair, so that all the felt is covered.

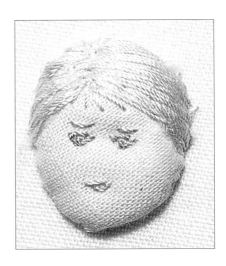

8. Work a running stitch 3mm (1/8in) round the outer edge of the completed head, leaving a loose tail. Remove the fabric from the hoop, then cut round the head, 3mm (1/8in) out from the running stitch. Pull up the loose thread to draw the calico behind the head shape, and fasten off.

If necessary, make two bullion knot ears (see page 29), one slightly longer than the other, on a line half way between the eyes and mouth.

Hands

I like to make hands that are quite detailed to mimic real ones. Individual fingers and thumbs are made by wrapping short lengths of paper-covered wire, then these are wrapped together to form palms and wrists. The fingers on the finished hand can then be bent to realistic shapes – the gardener's hand on page 76, for instance, is bent round the handle of a fork.

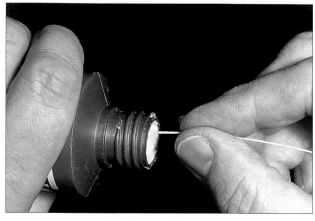

1. Cut the paper-covered wire into 50mm (2in) lengths (one length for each finger), then dip the end of one finger in PVA glue.

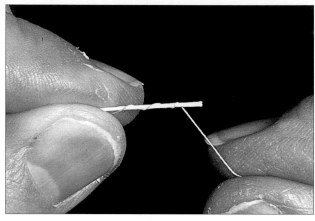

2. Starting approximately 20mm (¾in) from the end, loosely wrap a white thread down to the end of the wire.

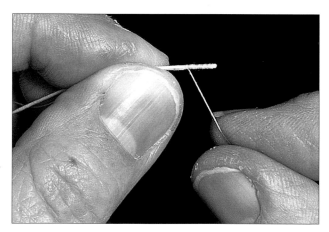

3. Now work back along the wire, closely wrapping the thread for approximately 12mm (½in). Add a touch more PVA glue if necessary to secure the thread to the wire. Leave a longish tail on each finger.

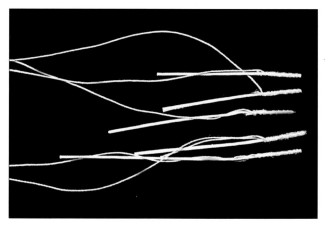

4. Repeat steps 1–3 for each finger and thumb.

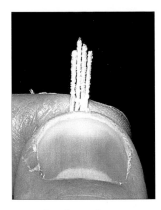

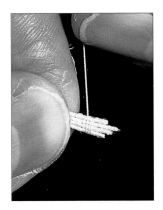

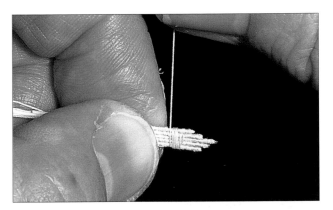

5. Take four fingers, and space them to mimic the length of those on your own hand.

6. Using one of the tails of thread, wrap the four fingers together for three or four turns to start to form the palm.

7. Place the wrapped-wire thumb beside the fingers, then continue wrapping thread down the palm.

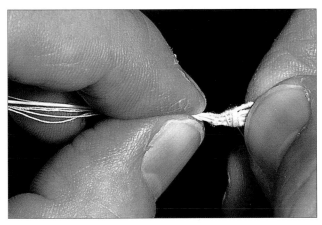

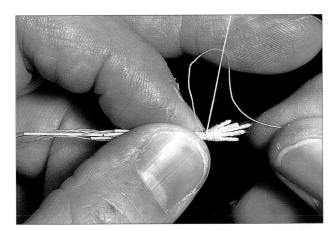

8. When the palm is complete, hold the fingers and thumb flat between two of your fingers, then squeeze the unwrapped wires together to form a wrist.

9. Now wrap the wrist and continue along the forearm for approximately 6mm (¼in). Fasten off the wrapping with one or two half-hitch knots.

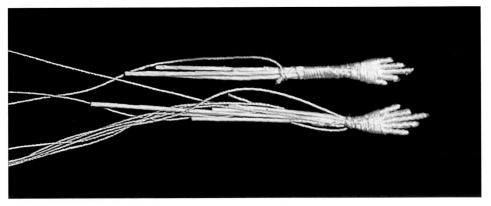

A pair of hands ready to be incorporated into an embroidery.

The Gardener

This picture of a man working in his garden includes lots of techniques, most of which are covered in the other projects in this book. If you want to make this embroidery, feel free to copy it exactly. Alternatively, you could use it as the basis for a more personal composition, and, say, depict the plants in your own garden. I used long and short stitch, French knots, satin stitch, raised stem stitch band, bullion knots, back stitch, and corded single Brussels stitch to complete this embroidery.

You will need:

Needlelace pads (see page 38)
Crochet thread No. 80
Sewing thread
Lightweight calico for the background fabric and slips
Fabric paints and brushes
Silk fabric
Iron-on interfacing
Salt
Cotton moulds
Six-stranded cotton
100/3 silk thread
No. 9 sharps needle
No. 10 ballpoint needle
No. 24 tapestry needle
Fine wire

Paper-covered wire
Acrylic paint
Beads
Toy stuffing
Felt
Double-knitting wool
Tubular ribbon
Organza
Air-drying clay
Cocktail stick
Stiletto
PVA glue
Metallic paint
Leather
Watering-can button

Enlarge this diagram to 150% to create a full-size pattern.

70

Painting the background

Paint the background (see page 63). Here I used a blue wash for the sky, a green wash for the grass and a brown wash for the earth. Leave a 'dry line' along the horizon and allow the sky wash to bleed down to this edge. Create the soft edge between the grass and earth by applying the brown wash while the green one is still damp. Leave the fabric to dry, then fix the colours with an iron.

Referring to the full-size pattern, use gold fabric paint to outline the shape of the gardener, the snail, the topiary and the tree trunk.

Espalier tree

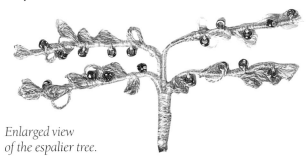

Enlarged view of the espalier tree.

This tree consists of lengths of paper-covered wire wrapped with silk and decorated with small beads. As you wrap the individual branches with silk, incorporate another type of thread and leave small loops to suggest leaves, and add the bead fruit along the length of the branch. Wrap the bottom ends of the branches together to form the trunk. Try to copy nature and make the finished trunk and the branches somewhat knobbly. Bend the branches to shape, then couch the tree on to the background fabric.

Cauliflowers and cabbages

There are six leaves on each of the two cauliflowers and on the cabbage. Each leaf is made from two layers of painted silk fabric, bonded together with iron-on interfacing, so the piece of silk needs to be large enough to provide thirty-six leaf shapes. Using a suitable shade of green, paint the silk fabric. When it is completely dry, cut it in half, then bond the two pieces together with iron-on interfacing.

Using the diagram below as a guide, back stitch the outlines of each leaf and its veins on the silk. Carefully cut out each leaf, just beyond the stitches, then, overlapping them slightly, stitch six leaves together on the background fabric.

Make a slip of French knots (see page 30) for the centre of each cauliflower, then sew these in the middle of the sets of leaves.

Paint a small piece of silk fabric dark green for the heart of the cabbage. While the paint is still wet, lightly sprinkle salt over the silk to create texture. When the silk is completely dry, brush off the salt, select an interesting area, then cut out a 50mm (2in) circle. Gather the fabric round a cotton mould, secure with a few oversewn stitches then trim off the excess fabric. Sew the finished cabbage heart to the circle of leaves.

Use this full-size diagram as a guide to cut the leaves for the cabbage and cauliflowers. Vary the shape slightly for each leaf, but keep them all at the same scale.

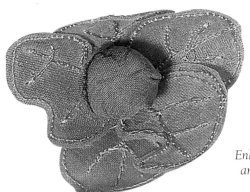

Enlarged views of the cabbage and one of the cauliflowers.

Pear tree

Working in the gold outline on the background fabric, use raised tem stitch band (see page 33) to embroider the tree trunk.

Use the cordonnet diagram to make fourteen needlelace leaves, using your choice of filling stitch. Reinforcing the outline of six leaves with fine wire, top stitch all round each leaf.

Use acrylic paint to colour pear-shaped beads. You could use medium-sized, round beads as apples or oranges.

Sew the nine background leaves to the background fabric. Here, leaves 1, 2 and 8 are not wired and sewn all round, whereas the other six are wired and are attached at their bases. Arrange the remaining five unwired leaves in a star-shape then secure this in the middle of the tree. Do not worry if these leaves curl up, they look quite natural this way.

Sew on the fruit beads then, finally, shape the freestanding parts of the wired leaves to make them look natural.

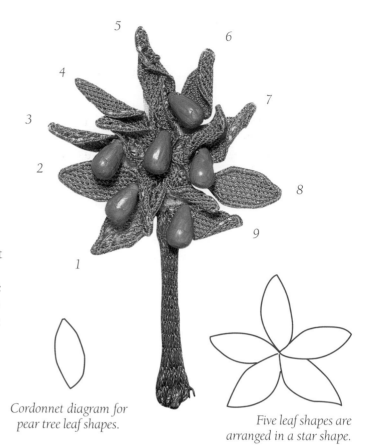

Cordonnet diagram for pear tree leaf shapes.

Five leaf shapes are arranged in a star shape.

Enlarged view of pear tree

Currants

Use the cordonnet diagram to make four needlelace leaf shapes, filling them with corded single Brussels stitch. Top stitch round the whole of each leaf shape.

The six currants are wrapped pebble beads. Using a long length of silk and a ballpoint needle, take the thread through the hole and round the outside of the bead until it is completely covered. Make joins by leaving all tails at one end of the bead (the base of the currant).

The tuft at the top of each currant is a short length of all strands of six-stranded cotton. Secure it by bringing a silk thread up through the bead, over the six strands and back down again. Trim the tuft to size.

Use one strand of six-stranded cotton to make the stalks. Tie a knot round all threads at the base of the currant, wrap the cotton thread round the other threads for approximately 12mm (½in), then fasten off.

Wrap a 40mm (1½in) length of paper-covered wire to make each stem. Incorporate the currants and leaves as you wrap the wire. Couch the base of the stems to the background fabric.

Enlarged view of currants.

Full-size cordonnet diagram for currant leaf shapes.

72

Marrow

Use the cordonnet diagrams to make the needlelace pieces for the marrow and the leaf.

Work the marrow shape as one piece. Fill the whole shape with a dark green corded single Brussels stitch, looping the stitches round the dividing lines. When the filling is complete, top stitch along the dividing lines with a pale green (do not top stitch round the outside edges). Release the needlelace, then sew the sides of the shape together to form a tube, leaving one end open. Fill the tube with toy stuffing, then close the end to complete the marrow.

Work the leaf segments in your choice of stitches, then top stitch round the outer edge. Sew the leaf to the background fabric, then secure one end of the marrow with a few stitches.

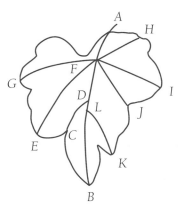

Full-size cordonnet diagram for the marrow leaf. This is rather more complex than any of the other cordonnets used in this book, but it is built up in a similar way to the leaf shape on page 39. Start with the loop in the cordonnet thread at point A, take both threads across to B and round to C. Take one thread up to D and back again, then take both threads round to E. Take one thread up to F and back again, then take both threads round to G. Continue working round the shape, using the double thread round the outer edge and taking one thread into the centre and back again for the side veins. At point K, take one thread down to B and back again, then take both threads to point L to finish the cordonnet.

Enlarged view of marrow.

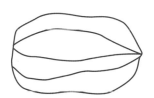

Full-size cordonnet diagram for the marrow. Work the shape as one piece, incorporating the cordonnet threads for the segments into the loops of the filling stitches.

Onions and carrots

Enlarged view of onions and carrots.

The onions are small wooden beads sewn to the background fabric. Bring a thread up through the fabric and the bead, take it over the bead and back down into the background fabric – repeat four or five times to securely attach the bead.

Cut a 150mm (6in) length of thread, wrap half of it round your finger, slip the loops off the finger and oversew the bottom of the loops twice. Now take the loose end of thread down through the bead and the background fabric, pull it firmly to draw part of the loops into the top of the bead, then fasten off on the back. Cut the loops in half to make the onion leaves.

The carrots are 3mm ($^{1}/_{8}$in) diameters of padded satin stitch (see page 35) sewn on to the background fabric. Wrap a 100mm (4in) length of thread round your finger, slip the loops off the finger, oversew them on top of the padded satin stitch, then cut the loops to form the leaves.

Strawberries

Four of the five strawberries are worked over stuffed felt, and consist of a decorated layer of needlelace. The freestanding strawberry comprises two decorated layers of needlelace, sewn together, then padded with toy stuffing.

Cut lengths of a pale gold thread, arrange them on the background fabric to represent straw, then couch them down with one or two stitches.

Enlarged view of the strawberries.

Full-size cordonnet diagrams for the strawberry and the calyx.

Full-size diagram for leaf shapes.

Referring to the pattern and the cordonnet diagram for the strawberry, cut four slightly undersize pieces of felt. Secure these to the background fabric, then pad them out with toy stuffing.

Use the cordonnet diagram to make six pieces of needlelace for the strawberries, filling each one with corded single Brussels stitch (see page 40). Before releasing these from the backing material, work a decorative layer of chain stitch into the needlelace. Then, using gold thread, make a small stitch over the securing stitch of the chain for the pips. Do not top stitch these pieces of needlelace. Sew four of the shapes over the padded felt. Sew the other two pieces together to make the freestanding strawberry, then pad this berry with toy stuffing.

Use the cordonnet diagram for the calyx to make six pieces of needlelace, filling each shape with corded single Brussels stitch. Top stitch round each shape, then remove it from the backing material. Secure the top edge of one shape to each of the padded-felt strawberries and two shapes to the freestanding berrys.

Wrap two lengths of paper-covered wire for the stalks. Secure one length to the freestanding strawberry, then take the other end of this through the background fabric and fasten off. Couch the other stalk across the top of the padded strawberries.

Use gold fabric paint to draw three leaf shapes on a piece of lightweight calico, spacing them slightly apart. Couch a length of fine wire round each leaf shape and down the centre vein, leaving a short tail at the base of each leaf. Fill in the shape with long and short stitch (see page 24). Buttonhole round the outside of each leaf and along their central veins. Define the side veins with straight stitches. Cut out each leaf, gather the wire tails together, then wrap them securely. Use a stiletto to make a hole in the background fabric, take the tail through the fabric and fasten it on the back.

Snail

Thread a strand of double knitting wool through a 150mm (6in) length of tubular ribbon. Sew one end of the ribbon in the middle of the shell shape on the background fabric, then coil the ribbon round this point, ending at the bottom of the shape. Make a bullion knot (see page 29) across the bottom of the shell for the body. Bring knotted lengths of thread up through the head to form the antennae, and trim to size.

Enlarged view of snail.

Butterfly

The wings of the butterfly sitting on one of the cauliflowers, are made in the same way as the one on pages 28–29, except that I use organza instead of lightweight calico as the background fabric. The body is a bullion knot.

Full size pattern and exploded view of the elements of the butterfly.

Topiary and pot

The topiary and its pot were made in much the same way as the project design on page 30. However, the trunk is a wrapped length of paper-covered wire, couched to the background fabric.

Fork

The tines of the fork are made from wrapped, paper-covered wire. The handle and shaft are made from a cocktail stick.

Cut two lengths of paper-covered wire – one 40mm (1½in) long, the other 25mm (1in) long – then wrap each length with grey silk. Bend each length into a 'U' shape, one slightly smaller than the other, then oversew the two shapes together, one inside the other to form four tines. Trim off any excess wire to equalise the tines.

Cut the points from the cocktail stick, then cut a 12mm (½in) length from one end for the handle. Use wood glue to stick the handle across the shaft and the tines to the bottom of the shaft. Leave to dry for at least twenty-four hours. Paint the handle and shaft with metallic paint, then leave it to dry.

Finally, carefully wrap the bottom of the handle, starting 6mm (¼in) up from the tines. At the bottom, reinforce the join between the tines and the handle with more wrapping. Put it to one side until the man is complete.

Flower bed

Paint pieces of silk fabric in the colours of your choice. When they are completely dry, cut each piece in half and bond together with iron-on interfacing. Cut the silk into 6mm (½in) circles to form the flower heads, then secure each to the background fabric with two or three stab stitches. Add a small bead or French knot in the centre of each flower. Make tufts of leaves in the same way as those for the onions and carrots, then sew these between the flowers. Fill in any gaps with more small beads and/or French knots.

Enlarged view of the flower bed.

Gardener

Use the exploded diagram below to make the cordonnets and needlelace shape for the clothes, filling each shape with corded single Brussels stitch. Work the hat in two pieces. Top stitch just the bottom edges of the jacket, the arm and the collar of the jacket, then release all the shapes from the backing material.

Cut slightly undersize pieces of felt for the man's legs, his body and his arm, and full size pieces of thin leather for the boots. Sew the felt legs shape to the background fabric, fill it with toy stuffing, then sew the needlelace trousers shape over the felt. Complete the legs by sewing the leather boots over the bottom of the legs. Sew the felt body shape to the background fabric, leaving the bottom edge open. Pad out the top part of this shape with toy stuffing, securing it with a few loose stab stitches (see page 19).

Now the head must be added. Here, the head is seen from the side, not the front, but the basic principles described earlier remain the same. Make a padded slip as shown on page 66 (step 3). Draw the head shape on to a piece of lightweight calico, then, starting at the top, back part of the head, sew it to the calico; work clockwise,

Full-size view of man.

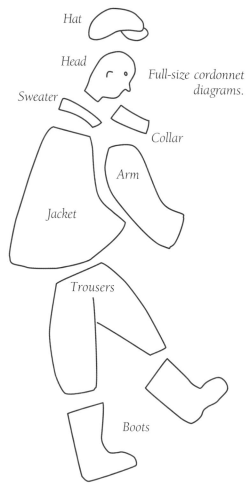

Hat

Head

Sweater

Full-size cordonnet diagrams.

Collar

Arm

Jacket

Trousers

Boots

carefully moulding the padded shape to the drawn outline to ensure you get a good contour, especially round the nose. Referring to the general instruction on page 6, add the eye, mouth, ear and hair. When you are happy with the head shape, work a running stitch 3mm (¹⁄₈in) round the outer edge, leaving a loose tail. Cut round the head, 3mm (¹⁄₈in) out from the running stitch. Pull up the loose thread to draw the calico behind the head shape, and fasten off. Sew the completed head to the top of the body shape, adding more padding if necessary.

Sew the needlelace sweater to the top of the body shape, ensuring that it covers the bottom of the head. Sew the jacket to the body shape, leaving the bottom edge free. This edge should just extend beyond the edge of the felt. Sew the collar to the top of the jacket.

Make one hand (see pages 68–69), leaving at least 25mm (1in) of wire for the arm, then sew the arm on to the background fabric and the body.

Cut a slightly undersize piece of felt for the arm, then sew this over the wired arm and body shape, taking the thread through the background fabric. Cover this with the needlelace arm, leaving the cuff edge free.

Sew the crown of the hat to the top of the head, then sew on its peak, leaving its bottom edge free.

Sew the fork to the background fabric, making two or three couching stitches over the top and bottom ends of the shaft. Mould the man's hand round the handle.

Finally, sew the watering-can bead to the background fabric.

The finished embroidery.

PATTERNS

These full-size patterns are for some of the
finished embroideries shown on the cover and
elsewhere in this book.

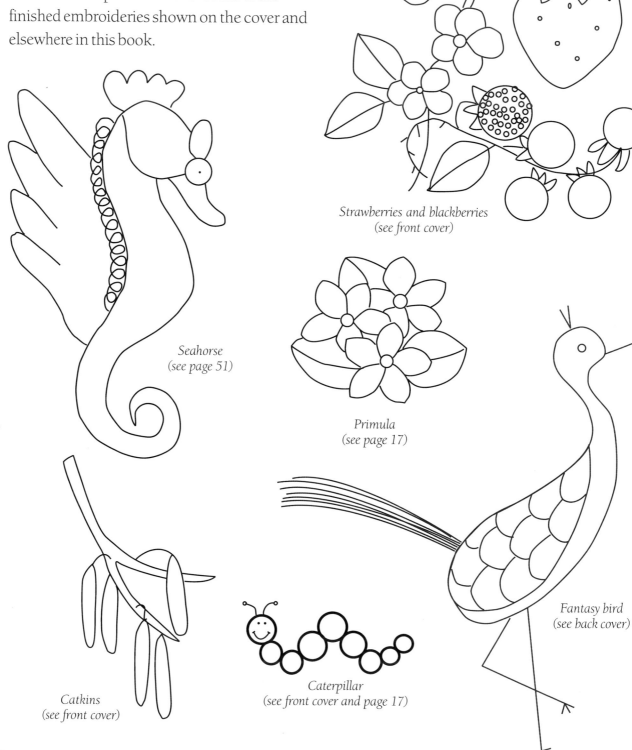

*Strawberries and blackberries
(see front cover)*

*Seahorse
(see page 51)*

*Primula
(see page 17)*

*Catkins
(see front cover)*

*Caterpillar
(see front cover and page 17)*

*Fantasy bird
(see back cover)*

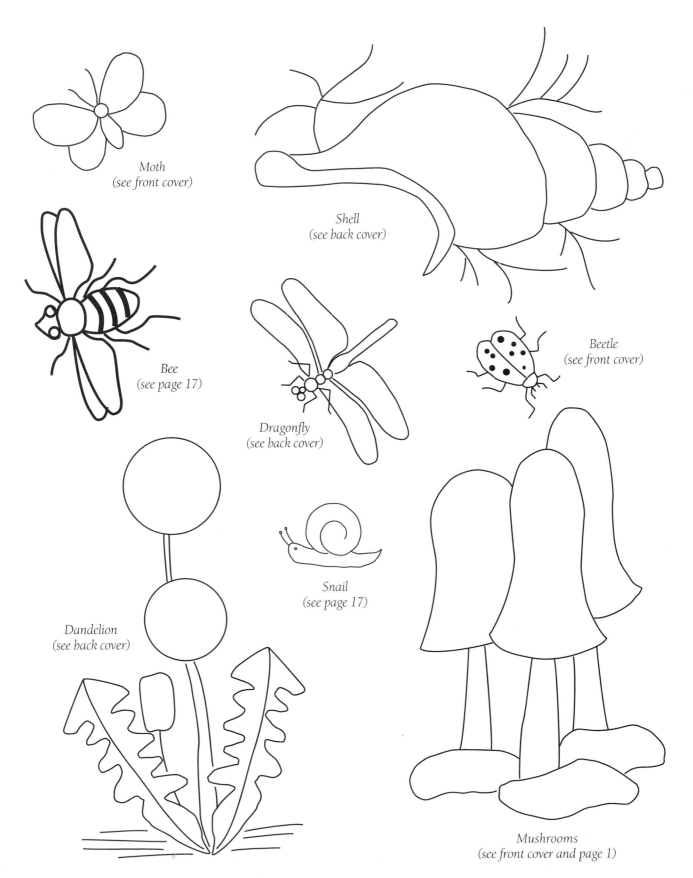

Moth
(see front cover)

Shell
(see back cover)

Bee
(see page 17)

Dragonfly
(see back cover)

Beetle
(see front cover)

Dandelion
(see back cover)

Snail
(see page 17)

Mushrooms
(see front cover and page 1)

INDEX